Theosophy

QUEST BOOKS
are published by
The Theosophical Society in America,
a branch of a world organization
dedicated to the promotion of brotherhood and
the encouragement of the study of religion,
philosophy, and science, to the end that man may
better understand himself and his place in
the universe. The Society stands for complete
freedom of individual search and belief.
In the Theosophical Classics Series
well-known occult works are made
available in popular editions.

Theosophy

A modern expression of the wisdom of the ages

BY ROBERT ELLWOOD

*This publication made possible with
the assistance of the Kern Foundation*

The Theosophical Publishing House
Wheaton, Ill. U.S.A.
Madras, India / London, England

The Theosophical Publishing House
306 West Geneva Road
Wheaton, Illinois 60189

A publication of the Theosophical Publishing
House,
a department of the Theosophical Society in
America.

Library of Congress Cataloging in Publication data.

Ellwood, Robert S., 1933-
   Theosophy: a modern expression of the wisdom
of the ages.

   (A Quest book)
   "A Quest original"—Verso t.p.
   Bibliography: p.
Includes index.
   1. Theosophy   I. Title.
BP565.E54T43   1986   299'.934   86-237
ISBN 0-8356-0607-4 (pbk.)

Printed in the United States of America.

Contents

About the Author

Robert Ellwood is Bashford Professor of Oriental Studies in the School of Religion at the University of Southern California. He has fourteen publications to his credit, including *Religious and Spiritual Groups in Modern America*, *Alternative Altars*, *Mysticism and Religions*, and two Quest books on meditation, *Finding the Quiet Mind* and *Finding Deep Joy*. A native of Normal, Illinois, he received his B.A. from the University of Colorado and his Ph.D. in the history of religions from the University of Chicago.

A Note on Sources

Volume and page references to the following works frequently cited in the text are to the following editions:

H. P. Blavatsky, *Isis Unveiled*, 2 vols. Wheaton, Illinois: Theosophical Publishing House, 1972.

———. *The Secret Doctrine**, Adyar edition, 6 vols. Adyar, Madras, India: Theosophical Publishing House, 1938, 1971. Also Collected Writing edition, 2 vols. plus index and bibliography. Adyar, Madras, India: Theosophical Publishing House, 1979.

———. *The Key to Theosophy*. London: Theosophical Publishing House, 1968.

A. T. Barker, transcriber and compiler, *The Mahatma Letters to A. P. Sinnett*, 3rd edition. Adyar, Madras, India: Theosophical Publishing House, 1979.

*NOTE: Volume and page references to *The Secret Doctrine* are given first to the Adyar edition (6 vols., 1938, 1971), followed by the Collected Writings edition (2 volumes plus index and bibliography, 1978), for example I:335/I:295.

Foreword

This book offers the treasures of that tradition of wisdom known as theosophy, as given in the writings of Helena P. Blavatsky and others, to the spiritual seekers of today's generation. It does not pretend to unveil all of those treasures, but it is hoped that enough is shown to encourage the reader to mine further the veins wherein they are to be found. Theosophy is, in the current phrase, "open-ended"; for every satisfaction it gives to spiritual or intellectual need, new vistas of wonder and new areas for inquiry open up behind that perception. A basic theosophical teaching is that we are perennially on pilgrimage; this is as true in the realms of intellectual quest and spiritual adventure as any other. For the true theosophist, it is in these realms that we are most truly human and at home. As the Upanishads of ancient India tell us, "Only in the Infinite is there joy." If this book can convey something of the wonder of such a vision of human reality, it will have achieved its greatest objective.

For me, the writing of the present volume has been something of a pilgrimage and voyage of discovery. I am not a theosophist of long-standing but one who has come in midlife to the study of this tradition, activated by the sense of cosmic and spiritual wonder it has evoked for me, and by a growing sense that in it many themes and queries that have long fascinated me converge. The composition of this book has been part of this journey. If it is successful in imparting any of the excitement of discovery I have experienced, I will be gratified; if in any way it is deficient, the reader must realize the voyage is still far from completed.

At the same time, the book is intended less as a personal statement than as a summary of theosophical teaching in the Blavatsky tradition, as it has developed in the Theosophical Society headquartered at Adyar, Madras, India. Its purpose has been to put the essence of this teaching in language able to convey it to modern readers without extensive background in theosophical studies. I have not avoided difficult areas or allusion to sometimes-controversial writers or ideas, for one objective has been to prepare readers for things they may find in the further study of theosophical literature, and to put them in the broad context of fundamental theosophical concepts. In this sense, this book is a survey of basic theosophical teaching in its fullness. When that teaching is even partially grasped, it evokes an amazingly rich vista of meaning in cosmic and human existence on many levels. Yet it must be understood that there are no "required" dogmas in theosophy; each inquirer is free to accept what seems reasonable and satisfying and leave the rest.

I am deeply indebted to the Kern Foundation for a grant which has made possible the writing of this book. I am likewise grateful to the National Education Committee of the Theosophical Society in America for the invaluable assistance its members have given by reading and commenting on the manuscript and by much-needed encouragement. The help and support of Dora Kunz, National President of the Theosophical Society in America, has been particularly appreciated. I am however solely responsible for the contents of this book, which in no way represents an official statement of the Society. One of the wonders of theosophical wisdom is that in its immensity it is capable of being approached from many different perspectives; these pages do not claim to be more than my own.

May an adventure of discovery begin as you turn the first pages of this or any theosophical book. For further information write The Theosophical Society in America, PO Box 270, Wheaton, IL 60189.

Introduction

What is your life really all about? Does some basic meaning underlie it, or is it just one thing after another amidst what William James called the "big, buzzing confusion" of the world?

These are questions about which we need to be very honest. It's easy to give stock answers. We may respond that we are here to experience, to love, to grow, to do something, to be tested, to win eternal life in heaven. All these answers are doubtless true as far as they go.

Nonetheless, deep queries can still remain. Such responses, however true, do not satisfy all the emptiness we can still feel in those dark hours when life seems to present itself to us as no more than a pointless journey from birth to death, a rocky excursion which never really delivers all it appears to promise in our early hopes and dreams, and around which all too soon the mists of old age, sickness, and death begin to gather.

As we see the follies and cruelties of the world around us, we ask ourselves why each generation seems to have to learn the same lessons over and over the hard way. Indeed, we wonder if each generation really exists for any purpose but to create and raise the next, which in turn produces the one after, over and over. We may be impelled by nature to the task, but to what end? Is there any sense in it at all? Or is it that by asking such questions, which presumably an animal would not ask, we just prove we are animals whose brains have outgrown their fleshly vehicles?

We fall back on the standard answers: go through this mess to experience, love, grow, get tested, win heaven. But the big question does not go away. Why does it have to be like this in the first place? Is this the only way to run a universe? Or is it all just some weird accident?

This book is about an ancient wisdom tradition called theosophy, revived in a modern form in the nineteenth century, which holds that the questions behind the questions can be properly asked, and answered. In the nature of things, the answers can never be absolute, but they can illumine basic principles which help one understand—and joyously live in— this very confusing, buzzing, and imperfect world.

This wisdom shows why, from the vantage point of one "at ground level" in our world, life in that world appears like little more than journeys from birth to death as generations follow one after the other. It enables us to understand the roles of suffering and joy in such a world, showing us that the contexts of our lives, in both space and time, are far deeper and more wonderful than we might have thought. It points to the significance of consciousness as a basic key to understanding reality and how this puts our tribulations and hopes in a new light. Minds—our own minds—are not just flashlights spotting a few scattered surfaces out there in a dark universe, but lamps that illumine its true nature from within.

In theosophical teaching, the fact that despite all its clutter the universe holds together at all means it must have some unifying principle. This tradition goes on to say that the fact that *we* are conscious means that consciousness must be an integral part of the universe, for *we are* parts of it, its children. Therefore we ought to be able to find out something of how the universe really works, not only by looking outside, as it were with a flashlight on a dark night, but also by looking deep within to discover our own nature. We can also find others who have already done so and are wise.

The journey inward is a long one—as long in its own way as would be an outward journey to the rim of the universe and the beginning of time. It is a journey requiring several steeds. Words and concepts are among them, but other mounts can traverse parts of the vast inner distances as well.

Before analyzing the others, let us look for a moment at one very important word, "theosophy" itself. This term comes from the Greek words *theos*, "god" or "the divine," and *sophia*, "wisdom." It means, therefore, "divine wisdom" or "wisdom about the divine."

To have wisdom is to know truth—important, beneficent truth. But truth does not have to be known in words, and the wise know that it can never be fully expressed verbally. Divine truth is an endless ocean, with cresting waves and still depths. As with the watery ocean that girds our planet, one knows it not only by studying oceanography but also by swimming, diving, and feeling its tangy spray, and not all the buckets in the world can begin to transport it.

Theosophy is about that kind of wisdom. It is wisdom concerning what that ancient Chinese classic, the *Tao Te Ching* of Lao-tzu, calls the Tao, the Way of the Universe; of the Tao, it says, "The Tao which can be spoken is not the real Tao," and again, "Those who know do not speak; those who speak do not know."

Yet such a statement cannot be taken absolutely. Those who know transmit wisdom in many ways other than words: in their eyes, in the way they walk and sit, and, we are told, in the dreams and inner visions of those they wish to teach. Nonetheless they often use words as well, aware that though a bucket cannot empty the ocean it can carry water, and (to change the image) that though words may not be the thing of which they speak, if they are the right words they at least point in the right direction.

Words are pointers. The old Zen saying tells us that when a finger is pointing at the moon (a symbol of Nirvana or complete enlightenment), you don't look at the finger but at the moon. But if the finger, which refers to words—in this case all the scriptures, doctrines, and lore of Buddhism—weren't there, you might not even realize the moon was in the sky, especially if it was behind a cloud bank or was that silvery ghost of a daylight moon which is there half the time, even though we usually give it no mind as we rush about our daily business here below.

Theosophy uses a lot of words and concepts (the two are inseparable) to point to that which is always there yet ultimately beyond words. The words are frail, no more adequate than is a finger compared to the cosmic immensities in which the moon wanders. Yet without words one might miss some pointers relevant to the big questions we all ask ourselves inwardly.

For we humans are question-asking creatures. Once in a Zen temple in Japan I saw a modern poster which translated said, "What is human life? Human life means asking 'What is human life?' " Much wisdom here. We are most truly human when we are most joyously or passionately asking the ultimate questions, and we most dehumanize ourselves when we set them aside, preoccupied as though drugged by gain, power, craving, or lazy dogmatism. But so much of the time we, like most of the world, operate under the influence of those opiates.

Theosophy comes out of a tradition which first of all holds (unlike some people) that such ultimate questions as what is human life can be asked, and on some levels significantly answered. It fully and frankly affirms that the great queries, "What is Reality? What is a human being? Where did we come from and where are we going? Why are our lives what they are?" can and must be asked, and that important "pointer" responses can be made to them.

In this respect theosophy is a profoundly positive and optimistic tradition, for it says there is meaning and it can be known. This implies a real underlying relationship between human life, words, ideas, and the infinite cosmos, which in itself tells us there is nothing to be pessimistic about in the last analysis. It says this relationship can be discovered in the most deeply human of activities, asking the right questions in a spirit of real concern and wonder.

The spiritual tradition which is theosophy is universal in the deepest sense, for there have been those in all times and places, undoubtedly, who have asked those questions and apprehended pointers. Evidence lies in the myths and religions, the symbols and lore of a thousand realms. But its most important articulations have been in Platonism and Neoplatonism in the West and in Vedanta and Buddhism in the East. They have been called Wisdom Traditions; they may also be called Wonder Traditions, for it is in the sheer sense of wonder at existence itself, at the ultimate mystery of why there is anything at all, that they begin.

Plato commented that philosophy (the "love of wisdom") begins with wonder, and that sometimes he was dizzy with amazement at the significance of things. Plotinus and the Neoplatonic tradition saw the universe as a chain of being extending from the One, and the One was not only supreme ineffable Reality but also supreme Beauty known in ecstasy.

Vedanta draws above all from those Vedic scriptures known as the Upanishads, which abound in a fresh, vibrant sense of the divine, Brahman, in all things and the joy this raises in the heart: Brahman is the youth and the maiden, the green parrot and the endless seas, and "only in the Infinite is there joy." According to the conventional account, Buddhism began when the Buddha, having seen an aged man, a dying man, and a corpse, began asking ultimate questions about the meaning of human life in the face of such suffering and wastage. Then after seeing a monk devoted to the spiritual quest, he knew he could give himself to none other than the same adventure, and he came to know within himself the sense of something unborn and undying, calm and self-sufficient, despite the change and decay of all things in the visible world.

The traditions of wisdom and wonder have been modified by the centuries, of course, in the West profoundly influencing Jewish, Christian, and Islamic mysticism and in the East becoming the many schools of Hindu and Buddhist thought. Yet in spite of variations they have retained several features born of the primordial wonder: an affirmation that an infinite divine reality—call it Brahman, God, or the One—underlies all that is and is the ultimate nature of all that is; that we humans, as part of it, have an infinite origin and destiny; and that these things can be known through wisdom, for they are our heritage and our very selves.

When the modern Theosophical Society was founded in New York in 1875 by Helena Blavatsky, Henry Steel Olcott, William Q. Judge, and others, it sought to reformulate this Ancient Wisdom from all these sources and other comparable teachings plus the instruction of living though hidden Masters. It is important to realize that modern theosophy was, and continues to be for those who are deeply attuned to it, an experience of wonder as well as of mere book learning, for wonder is still the pedagogue of true wisdom. The annals of the early days of the modern Theosophical Society impart this sense of wonder, for despite their many very human vicissitudes, this record leaves no doubt that the early theosophists felt they were experiencing extraordinary people and events as well as remarkable teachings. Above all Helena Blavatsky herself, the principal vehicle of the old/new lore, seemed herself to embody as well as to inculcate timeless mystery.

The French philosopher Gabriel Marcel made an important distinction between mysteries and problems. Problems are simply puzzles, like a mathematical calculation, that with enough time and skill can be fully solved. A mystery, however, can never be solved on a comparable level, because we ourselves are parts of it; we can only experience it in our lives and grow toward understanding from within, as it were.

Questions about the ultimate nature and meaning of reality and human destiny, which I have already noted are basic to the wisdom or wonder tradition, are such mysteries. They cause one to ask questions and to ask them in the largest possible context; if an answer is given, it is an answer that is an experience as well as a solution.

In the word "theosophy," the term *theos*, god, can be taken to mean our ultimate environment, infinite Reality itself. We talk a great deal about environment today, and rightly so, for there is no more fundamental realization than that the existence of anything is always an existence within a context, an environment. The atom, the molecule, the cell, the body, the community, the planet, the solar system—all are in intimate and necessary relation to each other and to that which is larger than they. The greater could not exist without the smaller, nor the smaller without the larger system that shapes it. Specialized cells do not come into being without bodies, nor planets without suns, and cosmologists generally believe that atoms and molecules can exist only in the space-time continuum of a universe. Nature creates nothing singly —if there is one star, waterfall, or animal of a species, there are many—and nothing is created without an environment with which it is in interaction.

Our ultimate environment is infinite Reality itself. It is also our closest environment, for it is manifested in everything, including ourselves. We can exist only in deep interaction with it, as with all our other environments. It is *theos*.

The means for that interaction is *sophia*, wisdom, the other half of "theosophy." *Sophia* is not just puzzle-solving knowledge but mystery-understanding, insight, *prajna* in the Sanskrit term, which knows because it grasps in a single flash the total pattern and the whole web of interactions that make up a situation. To put it another way, *sophia* is holistic. It sees the situation in connection with its whole series of environmental sheaths, right up to its relation to its ultimate environment, infinite Reality itself.

Gaining wisdom, then, means expanding horizons, seeing things in larger and larger frameworks, until all frames whatsoever fall away and we see all as infinite Reality. How do we expand horizons? Through what in the theosophical tradition, and many others, are called initiations.

Life is a series of asking questions and a series of initiations. The two go together. The child asks what it is like to be adult and in time is initiated by a series of expanding experiences into adulthood.

The basic characteristic of an initiation is that it is, in a term of closely related meaning from ancient times, a mystery. That word in turn comes from a Greek word meaning keeping silent, for it refers to that which cannot truly be spoken in words but only experienced with one's whole self. In Marcel's sense, it brings us into something which can be known only by life-experience, not by problem-solving alone.

The fundamental initiatory experience is at the heart of all great spiritual rites and transitions—death and rebirth. It is a death to one kind of life, and a birth to another in which one is more widely aware, in significant rapport with a larger environment.

Though the child, then, may ask what it is like to be an adult, the verbal answers one can assimilate as a child do not add up to wisdom about adulthood. That comes only after, through a series of biological and social initiations, he dies to the life of a child and is reborn as an adult, a person with wider horizons and wider capabilities on both the biological and social levels.

Here we may note two kinds of initiations. What may be called natural initiations are those we pass through just because we are human beings transiting human life: birth, puberty, adulthood, parenthood, old age, death.

Various cultures also design social initiations, often in conjunction with natural initiations. These help individuals through the natural initiations in ways compatible with the society's values. They put natural transitions in a sacred context, such as those initiating young men and women into adulthood. These are often programmed to bring out very dramatically the death and rebirth aspects of the rite, with candidates perhaps being sealed in a lodge, or even semiburied, at the heart of the rite; the candidates may at this time expect to see visions and hear voices of gods as tokens of expanding awareness.

Social initiations can also be individual, undertaken voluntarily—or in response to a personal divine call. People voluntarily undertook the initiations of the ancient "mystery religions," like those of Eleusis or Isis, as today they become initiated into lodges, fraternities, religious orders, priesthoods, or discipleships. Like all initiations, the scenarios may offer the candidate powerful sensory and subjective experience which help awaken new kinds of knowing and aid one to see individual life in the context of newly appreciated spiritual environments.

In addition to natural and social initiations, theosophy, like most spiritual traditions, affirms what may be called inner initiations. These follow no obvious biological or social program but have a dynamic of their own—or rather, a dynamic linked to one's past and present web of interactions with the larger environment in ways too subtle to be seen save with the eye of wisdom. In this kind of initiation, one passes through inner death and rebirth experiences and realizes inner awakenings to broader horizons and new dimensions of one's material and spiritual environments. One may, of course, stimulate such initiations through practices like prayer and meditation which make one especially accessible to them; yet they usually come with seeming spontaneity. In classic spiritual writings, they are represented by such stages of inner growth as illumination, the dark night of the soul, and the unitive state.

Theosophy tells us that initiatory growth is not limited to this life alone but is an ongoing process of "the pilgrim," the "monad" or "soul" over countless lifetimes whose beginning and end we can scarcely imagine. The greatness and vastness of the theosophical universe, which even modern cosmology only begins to approach (though it corroborates it on significant levels) is indeed evocative of the wonder with which wisdom begins—and ends.

In particular, we are told that there are those, often called Adepts, Mahatmas, or Masters, who have evolved spiritually well beyond the ordinary human level. This means that they are less visible than ordinary humans, for they have merged into a larger part of the environment; they are from our perspective "part of the background." Yet out of their great compassion, which is part of spiritual growth, they are concerned about struggling humanity and in subtle ways guide the evolution of the planet and of individuals. They have the capacity to do this because every initiation, from birth on the natural level on up to the inner spiritual initiation of a high adept, gives one knowledge in a larger context, knowledge about a wider and subtler environment. It also brings (in the Buddhist term) skill-in-means, ability to use expanded horizons of knowledge in accordance with wisdom and compassion. The Masters are very far advanced along these lines.

A larger context is what practical theosophy is about. Take for example our own times, the twentieth century. How can we possibly understand such an era, such an experience as our century's, just in itself? Like many another age, "It was the best of times, it was the worst of times," but both to wildly extreme degrees. Millions have known prosperity, health, and mechanized luxury of which previous generations could have hardly dreamed. Millions more caught up by Hitler's death camps, Cambodian genocide, famine and drought and numerous other twentieth-century horrors have found that the human capacity for evil and suffering did not diminish in the face of the century's "progress." This century began with the horse and buggy and ended with the spaceship and the computer, while the population of the globe doubled twice.

How can we comprehend such times? The Earth can be really understood only as part of the solar system and the universe, and a person's life at, say, forty-five can only be understood with reference to the childhood, youth, and young adulthood that went before and the aging that will follow. So, theosophical teaching suggests, a century—and the whole human experience on this planet—does not interpret itself but can only be interpreted as the wisdom eye looks at in relation to larger and larger environments. Human history, according to theosophy, is not to be understood solely from the perspective of this planet but in relation to the solar system and the universe as a whole, nor is it to be understood solely in terms of the peoples now walking its stage.

We will look at the details of these matters later. Now it is enough to open up the sense of wonder, the immensely large perspective, of theosophical thought. It helps us to live in our age if we understand that while we belong to the world we inhabit —for we were drawn to it by deep webworks of affinity—we also have come from elsewhere and go elsewhere, and no one age or world can answer all our needs or fulfill all our potential.

A moment's introspection may confirm the inner truth of these parallel realities. We are often tempted to think we deserve a better world than this one with all its appalling cruelty, hatred, and injustice. Yet if we are honest with ourselves, we are likely to realize that these things are not wholly alien to our own nature, that we have within ourselves at least the roots of the evil we see around us. We also harbor cruel, greedy, and selfish thoughts.

At the same time, our sense of alienation from the world is also a real part of us bearing its own truth. We are not *just* of this world at this particular point in its history. Though we have been drawn to it, we also have potential for more and are capable of initiations by which we can disidentify with it save to serve it with compassion. *In theosophy, consciousness is a fundamental reality.* Worlds and human lives are ultimately the outward expression of states of consciousness. They are stages in developing expression of consciousness, large and small, in interaction with matter. They come together as like seeks like.

Yet one is not bound to the place where one finds oneself but can seek initiation into a new and better state, ultimately a new and better world. But one must never forget that it is not by seeking such things *for oneself*, getting enlightened without concern for everyone else, that they are found. It is rather through losing oneself in compassionate service that one finds, almost without knowing it, freedom from the world.

This is the kind of wisdom theosophy teaches. Before going on to examine it in more specific terms, a final question must be asked: How do we know it is true?

While as we have seen that theosophy does not claim more than to point toward truth, knowing that full truth is greater than language, it does claim that its pointers are of some value in apprehending that truth of which the motto of the Theosophical Society speaks when it says, "There is no religion higher than truth." The tradition affirms, too, that living a life in accordance with theosophical wisdom can prepare one for initiation into the experiential dimensions of higher spiritual reality.

The question of how we know can be answered on three levels. We will be dealing more fully with these responses throughout this book, but it may be useful just to cite them here.

First, the historical level. Theosophists have long contended that extraordinary aspects of the production of the modern theosophical classics, such as Helena P. Blavatsky's *Isis Unveiled* and *The Secret Doctrine*, suggest a larger purpose behind their offering to the world. (See the Appendix of this book for a summary of the history and literature of modern theosophy.) Nevertheless, theosophists tend to agree that ultimately this literature must speak for itself independently of how it came into being in our time.

Second, independent judgment can be made on the basis of sound reason and science. Theosophists would hold that their basic premises—the ultimate unity of all reality and the interaction of all entities with larger environments in spatial and temporal webs of cause and effect and the inseparability of consciousness from the universe's manifestations—can be arrived at on quite rational grounds and require no "mystical" modes of knowing. They find, also, that while some of theosophy's teachings go beyond what empirical science now knows or perhaps can know (such as the prehistory of the consciousness now embodied in human beings on Earth), in its broad outlines theosophy is not inconsistent with scientific knowledge and seems in fact more and more to fit the general view of reality toward which cosmology is moving.

Finally and most important, a fundamental theosophical principle is that truth has a self-revelatory and self-validating quality. It goes like this. If there is an ultimate truth or ultimate reality about the universe, as there must be since the cosmos has some sort of unity and constancy, that truth must be revealed to human beings, or knowable by human beings, in some way. For we, with our consciousnesses, are part of the universe; we came out of it and all that we are is latent in it and of the same nature as the universe. We must assume, then, that somewhere in human life significant truth about the nature of the reality of which we are children can be known by our instrument of knowing, consciousness. Since humans differ and obviously are not all of absolutely equal mental power, this knowledge would not be equally known by all or accessible to all. Yet since all human groupings and cultures have people of high ability as well as otherwise, this knowledge should be revealed in some form in all corners of the Earth. But it concerns an ultimate reality to which, as we have seen, words and concepts can only point. It would not be surprising, then, if the outward form of those pointers differed in various cultures and geographies. So it would seem to be if one looked out impartially over the many myths and symbols of the human spiritual world, and so the theosophical tradition says it is.

Theosophy holds that behind the symbols and languages of the world's manifold religions lies a common pattern of pointers to ultimate truth. That inner pattern is more wisdom than puzzle-solving, for it is fully understood only through initiations. It is thus doubly veiled; it is hidden behind outer signs and tokens, and it is knowable only in the context of consciousness-expanding experiences or initiations. In theosophy this inner wisdom is called "esoteric," "occult," "the ancient wisdom," and "the secret doctrine."

These words do not mean it is only for an elite. It is not undemocratic; it is in principle accessible to all, and its power, as it works through the forms of the various religions, can be tapped for good by the humblest. Theosophists want nothing more than for it to be known to all, to be "unsecret." It is rather hidden from some at first by its own nature—the wisdom is universal, yet humanity is divided into many tribes and cultures. Wisdom's outward expression therefore varies, and so to get into it one must crack its codes. Further, as wisdom it requires that one approach it as one approaching a mystery. To truly *know*, one must be prepared for knowing through life-experience and life-transformation, through initiation. Many want to know facts but not all want to change in the process, yet there are facts which can be known only very partially and perhaps misleadingly, like the child's knowledge of adulthood, without concomitant initiation.

Unlike some mysteries or initiations, theosophical growth does not require undergoing a formal external rite in order to get in touch with the ancient wisdom. Study itself—reading theosophical books, hearing theosophical lectures—together with proper spiritual preparation through devotion to service and a free, tranquil mind, can be initiatory experiences that expand horizons and lead to wisdom. Such initiations as are needed will be imparted inwardly by those guiding the evolution of the Earth, or of the particular individual.

Let us then turn to a consideration of basic theosophical teaching, with the hope that for those who read, as for the one who writes, the experience will begin to open the door of wisdom.

1
Theosophical Foundations

Theosophical wisdom points to realities exceeding the power of human words and concepts. Yet it employs words, for it indicates that the answers to the problems of human existence do lie, so to speak, in certain directions. Some ideas which can be put into words—Oneness, the interaction of consciousness and matter, periodicity or the recurrence of cycles, karma or cause-and-effect, for instance—do get at the really deep structures underlying what we experience much better than other ideas. While there are no cast-in-cement dogmas, theosophical discussion keeps coming back to certain basic topics such as these.

Modern writers in the theosophical tradition have made various lists of basic concepts. They all differ somewhat in wording, but readers will also be struck by a high degree of repetition. This suggests two things. First, that there are, indeed, some core ideas held by most people in the theosophical tradition. Second, the difference in wording and in the exact scope of the lists shows that the way theosophy is understood and expressed is always an individual matter. Let us now examine some of these basic ideas.

First we might look at three fundamental propositions basic to H. P. Blavatsky's *The Secret Doctrine*. Briefly stated, they are as follows:

1. An Omnipresent, Eternal, Boundless and Immutable PRINCIPLE, on which all speculation is impossible, since it transcends the power of human conception and could only be dwarfed by any human expression or similitude. It is beyond the range and reach of thought—in the words of the Mandukya [Upanishad], "unthinkable and unspeakable."

2. The Eternity of the Universe *in toto* is a boundless plane, periodically "the playground of numberless Universes incessantly manifesting and disappearing," called "the manifesting stars" and the "sparks of Eternity." "The Eternity of the Pilgrim" is like a wink of the Eye of Self Existence . . ." "The appearance and disappearance of Worlds is like a regular tidal ebb of flux and reflux."

3. The fundamental identity of all Souls with the Universal Oversoul, the latter being itself an aspect of the Unknown Root; and the obligatory pilgrimage for every Soul—a spark of the former—through the Cycle of Incarnation (or "Necessity") in accordance with cyclic and karmic law, during the whole term. (Summarized from I:79-82/I:14-17.)

Building from this magnificent statement, we shall now list a few points which will be central to our approach to theosophy.

A. One infinite and incomprehensible Reality underlies and unites all that is or can ever be. It expresses itself through consciousness and matter, so that all phenomena represent the complex interaction of these two.

B. Universes, solar systems, and worlds develop through immense cycles in accordance with the dynamics of this interaction.

C. The individual human being, sometimes called "The Pilgrim," moves through these universes and worlds lifetime after lifetime in response to karma and the necessity of experiencing many kinds of being, before returning to the Source, the One.

D. There is a reservoir of wisdom in our world, known to those well advanced on the path but accessible to all earnest seekers, that can help us to understand and grow in these truths.

E. Growth is not only a matter of intellectual learning but involves also initiation or inward transformation and living in accordance with the spirit of openness and the oneness of all being that the truth implies.

Another list which ought to be taken into account, though of a different nature from the foregoing, are the "Three Declared Objects" of the Theosophical Society which are published in most of its documents and periodicals. These are important because they illustrate the difference, and interrelationship, between the "consensus" theosophical teaching about the nature of humanity and the universe (indicated in what we have presented) and the concrete role of the Theosophical Society. The Objects are:

1. To form a nucleus of the Universal Brotherhood of Humanity, without distinction of race, creed, sex, caste, or color.

2. To encourage the study of Comparative Religion, Philosophy, and Science.

3. To investigate unexplained laws of Nature and the powers latent in man.

The only intellectual commitment expected of people wishing to affiliate with the Theosophical Society is that they declare themselves "in sympathy" with these objects. No philosophical or theological doctrine is mandated, not even a concept as fundamental to the "consensus" as Oneness and the omnipresence of consciousness. Rather, one is simply encouraged to study comparative religion, philosophy, and science, and to investigate unexplained laws of nature and powers latent in man, both individually and in concert with the Society.

The theosophical tradition has confidence that if one pursues these studies and investigations with sufficient honesty and depth, one will come to realize, in one's own way, the Oneness of the universe, the inner significance of consciousness, and the other broad consensus points of the tradition. But the crucial matter to be understood is that these are truths that one *must* learn for oneself and are never rightly appropriated simply as dogmas. One who takes them merely on the authority of others, or of an institution, does not really begin to comprehend them, even if that person uses all the "right" words.

Second, we see in the first Object a program which puts the consensus ideas, very broadly conceived, into practical application. For theosophy teaches that the unity of the universe is its most basic reality, consciousness is always intertwined with appearances, and all humanity is on the same great path. How could this be expressed socially but in ways that emphasize the universal brotherhood of humanity and that make no distinction on grounds of race, creed, sex, caste, or color? Of this natural brotherhood the Theosophical Society forms a nucleus. To worldly eyes this Society doubtless seems small and insignificant before the immense divisions and inequalities which still beset the race. Yet, small as it is, it is still an organization which, more than many larger ones, is interracial, cross-cultural, cross-creedal, and committed to sexual equality. A nucleus does not have to be large in comparison to that of which it is nucleus, or even at the precise center; like a kernel of grain or, say, the nucleus of an art collection, it merely has to show the direction of authentic growth and facilitate that growth, not be the whole collection. Its members believe that the Theosophical Society is quietly doing its work in that respect and that its consensus teachings explain why only "Universal Brotherhood" can be the true destination of the human adventure.

THE OMNIPRESENCE OF CONSCIOUSNESS

We must now get back to the basic features of the consensus. After Oneness, the most important point is that observed reality is the interplay of consciousness and matter, of which outward forms are but reflections. If we ask what it is that effectively unites all existence, it would be the link between consciousness and matter. That link holds near and far, past and future, together in a single thought. It is the force that binds all things together.

Consciousness, then, is everywhere we see space, time, and form at all. We may, in a commonsense way, think that some things like rocks and clouds are matter only. At the atomic level, however, even the solidest rock dissolves away into pure energy, and this, says wisdom, betokens the interaction of consciousness and its material counterpart, the two inseparable expressions of the fundamental reality at the core of what seems pure matter.

The Secret Doctrine tells us further that time "is only an illusion produced by the succession of our states of consciousness as we travel through Eternal Duration, and it does not exist where no consciousness exists in which the illusion can be produced, but 'lies asleep.'" Eternal Duration, we are told, is not time as we think of it, but a process in which ever-real idea-forms pass through a "mathematical line" known as the present, into the "region of memories that we name the Past." Only a kind of blurring in the mind gives us the sensation of temporal duration. (I:110/I:37)

It may be pointed out that this picture of the universe and mind converges remarkably with the holographic model of the universe proposed by Karl Pribram of Stanford in the 1970s. A holograph is a three-dimensional representation or picture made by reflecting light off a photographic plate which has been imprinted with the holograph, or code, by a laser beam together with light bounced off the object to the pictured. A key characteristic of a hologram is that all parts of it contain the whole; if broken, the entire picture can be reproduced in less detail from any fragment.

Pribram concluded that the brain operates by a sort of holographic process; it constructs reality by creating holographic images within itself from frequencies (ideal forms?) that have no time or space reality of their own. The primary order of the universe, then, is not actual space, time, or substance, but nondimensional waves prior to these, which the mind interprets holographically as material reality. Ultimately, then, the universe would not be made up of entities localized in space and time, this star here and that one there, an event now and another a million years in past or future. As in Blavatsky's Eternal Duration, all possibilities are present all the time, latent in every part of the universe as in a holographic code, ready to be reproduced from any fragment of it—including the fragment which is a human brain.

The universe and its history, and our own life-stories, then, are simply images we are creating and stories we are telling ourselves from out of the holographic frequencies in our minds, in accordance with our particular principle of selectivity from the infinite array of images available. For the mind, in Henri Bergson's term, works as a reducing valve, ordinarily able to channel only a tiny bit of the endless sensory and other sensations available.

From the theosophical point of view, the particular world each of us creates from out of the unimaginable range of holographic codes available is based on affinity, or (in the theosophical term we shall soon discuss more fully) karma.

In passing, let us observe that in this model of the universe no theoretical objection exists to psychic phenomena such as clairvoyance (awareness of events far away), precognition (knowledge of future events), retrocognition (perception of past scenes in present time), or telepathy. For near and far, past and future would all be amenable to holographic reproduction from every fragment of space and time, if (so to speak) the light hits it right or the receiving mind can tilt itself the right way. While not the central focus of theosophy, such phenomena have always been accepted by the tradition as significant, since they offer clues to the true nature of reality and have played important roles in the history of the Ancient Wisdom.

Theosophists are not bound to Pribram's or any other model of reality, whether from religion, philosophy or the physical sciences, being aware that such models come and go as human thought develops. Models from one's own time which show a convergence with the spirit of the tradition can, however, serve as metaphors which help in understanding, just as theosophical language itself should be regarded as mere pointing toward the truth not truth itself.

In this case, though, both views appear to be pointing to a concept that all existence is unified in the truly radical sense that it is all finally the timeless and spaceless stuff of "raw" consciousness and matter, processed by "minds" to produce the apparent universe. Blavatsky, as usual, puts it well: The universal process is "the only universal and eternal *reality* casting a periodical reflection of *itself* on the infinite Spatial depths. This reflection, which you regard as the objective *material* universe, we consider as a temporary *illusion* and nothing else." Personalities, she says in a striking illustration, are like the sudden flashes of the Northern Lights, "as real as can be while you look at it," yet also an illusion for (as in all reality) nothing tangible is there, the lights are not as real as the forces which produced them. (*Key*, 84-85)

Or as *The Secret Doctrine* puts it:

> Nothing is permanent except the one hidden absolute Existence which contains in itself the noumena of all realities. The existences belonging to every plane of being, up to the highest Dhyan Chohans,* are, comparatively, like the shadow cast by a magic lantern on a colorless screen. Nevertheless all things are relatively real, for the cognizer is also a reflection, and the things cognized are therefore as real to him as himself. (I:113/I:39)

This illusion/reality is called Maya, the Sanskrit term, which is, incidentally, related to our word

---

*Divine Intelligences charged with supervision of the cosmos.

magic, suggesting that the visible universe is akin to a magician's show. As we grow in development, we realize more and more the real nature of its sleights-of-hand, though for long the process may mean only the replacement of one mayavic image for another. This way to realization is called in India *Jnana Yoga*, the way of meditation using intellectual analysis. Helena Blavatsky put the matter strikingly in a discourse given in the last year of her life, preserved as follows in notes taken by Commander Robert Bowen, a student of hers.

> As one progresses in Jnana Yoga, one finds conceptions arising which, though one is conscious of them, one cannot express nor yet formulate into any sort of mental picture. As time goes on these conceptions will form into mental pictures. This is a time to be on guard and refuse to be deluded with the idea that the new found and wonderful picture must represent reality. It does not. As one works on, one finds the once admired picture growing dull and unsatisfying, and finally fading out or being thrown away. This is another danger point, because for the moment one is left in a void without any conception to support one, and one may be tempted to revive the cast-off picture for want of a better to cling to. The true student will, however, work on unconcerned, and presently further formless gleams come, which again in time give rise to a larger and more beautiful picture than the last. But the learner will now know that no picture will ever represent the TRUTH. This last splendid picture will grow dull and fade like the others. And so the process goes on, until at last the mind and its pictures are transcended and the learner enters and dwells in the World of NO FORM, but of which all forms are narrowed reflections.
>
> The true student of *The Secret Doctrine* is a Jnana Yogi, and this Path of Yoga is the True Path for the Western student. It is to provide him with

sign posts on that Path that *The Secret Doctrine* has been written. (From notes recorded by Robert Bowen in 1891 from lectures by H. P. Blavatsky. Published in Ianthe H. Hoskins, ed., *Foundations of Esoteric Philosophy from the Writings of H. P. Blavatsky.* London: Theosophical Publishing House, 1980, pp. 66-67.)

We can see that, if all arises from consciousness interacting with matter then clearly all is alive, and there is no dead matter or wholly disembodied spirit. In this interplay, all forms are seen as but stages of development. From this starting point, all the other concepts of theosophy will fall into place.

It is important to underscore that theosophy is not some form of metaphysical idealism or mentalism which says that consciousness is *prior* to matter, or that what we see of the material world is no more than a projection of mind having no reality apart from mind. Misconceptions on this score are all too easy, for theosophy does speak of consciousness as being everywhere, and of everything we see, however "material" it appears, as shaped by consciousness. But matter in some form is always present; without it, consciousness would have nothing to shape and nothing to respond to in its creative activity. It would be as empty as matter without spirit. What is prior is not consciousness as we know it but the Unknown Root from which both consciousness and matter stem. Thus, the universe is a great concourse of interconnected being, matter and spirit, larger and smaller, inner and outer. In a much-quoted passage from *The Secret Doctrine*:

> From Gods to men, from Worlds to atoms, from a Star to a rush-light, from the Sun to the vital heat of the meanest organic being—the world of Form and Existence is an immense chain, the links of which are all connected. The Law of Analogy is

the first key to the world problem, and these links have to be studied coordinately in the Occult relations to each other. (II:328/I:604)

INSIDE AND OUTSIDE

Let us think in other ways about consciousness as omnipresent. What is this universe in which we pilgrims find ourselves? We know it in two ways: what we see with our eyes looking outward and what we experience from within. The two aspects are very different. One way is essentially seeing surfaces, whether still or moving. Looking at a human surface involves trying to intuit what is going on inside from the way it moves, configures its visage, and makes noises. The other way of knowing the universe, experiencing from within, is very different. It is sensing awareness and feeling firsthand but never being quite sure how the surface looks, for the eye cannot see itself directly, and we have not the gift to see ourselves as others see us.

It is easy, of course, to assume that the outward vision is the more reliable. It sees far more of the universe's expanse than the inner. It can be measured, analyzed, and predicted. Yet doubts linger. Apart from me, and what I can intuit in other humans, has the universe only an outside? Can I ever know what it *really* is in itself, just by seeing its surfaces?

I realize also that however much of the universe I can see outwardly, aided by telescopes and microscopes, it can never be more than the tiniest fragment of what is, whether the smallest organism or a billion other worlds.

Blavatsky wrote:

> Finite reason agrees with science, and says: "There is no God." But, on the other hand, our

Ego, that which lives and thinks and feels independently of us in our mortal casket, does more
than believe. It *knows* that there exists a God in nature, for the sole and invincible Artificer of all
lives in us as we live in Him. No dogmatic faith or
exact science is able to uproot that intuitional feeling inherent in man, when he has once fully realized it in himself (*Isis* I, 36).

God here can be taken to be the universal Unknown Root, and the Ego the inner manifestation of
it as consciousness, which in the last analysis knows
its true identity as surely as the outer self believes it
knows its name. One way, therefore, remains to
know what the universe really is: not to look outward
at surfaces, but to look inward at the one sample or
test case of the *inward* nature of the universe available to each of us, our own selves. Here we find the
reality of consciousness as fundamental as that of
matter: its external features, even thoughts and
dreams, are but outward-moving expressions. We
may come to realize from analogy with our own case
that:

The Universe is worked and *guided*, from *within*
outwards. As above, so it is below, as in heaven, so
on earth; and man, the microcosm and miniature
copy of the macrocosm, is the living witness to
this Universal Law and to the mode of its action
(*The Secret Doctrine* I:317/I:274).

Just as we are guided from within out—our invisible minds moving our arms and legs—so is the universe as a whole.

The Secret Doctrine teaches: the fundamental
identity of all Souls with the Universal Oversoul,
the latter being itself an aspect of the Unknown
Root; and the obligatory pilgrimage for every Soul

—a spark of the former—through the Cycle of In-
carnation, or Necessity, in accordance with the
Cyclic and Karmic Law, during the whole term.
(*The Secret Doctrine* I:82/I:17).

The individual, then, is consciousness particularized in interaction with matter, consciousness set
apart for purposes of pilgrimage. One could say it is
done with mirrors. (In *The Voice of the Silence* Blavatsky says "mind is like a mirror.") The universe is
like a magic hall of mirrors in which the reality of
each entity, each Pilgrim, depends on the way he reflects all the other mirrors from a particular angle.
This angle gives each of us the special uniqueness we
rightly prize. Yet it is nothing we *have* but something
which, like reflected light, we are able to *give* in a
particular way. And each angle of reflection shifts
over the aeons as the light grows brighter and
brighter in the mirror.

We have already alluded to another aspect of the
particularization of consciousness which is not unre-
lated to evolution: the establishment of affinities. The
monadic mirror-consciousnesses are drawn to one
another through similarities in the world that each
creates by its filtering from the universal hologram.
Those finding more or less the same world, then, discover themselves making and experiencing it together. For example, those of us who have brought ourselves to a stage in the endless pilgrimage offered by
this planet called Earth, with its day and night, pleasure and pain, hope and despair—and who this time
around have been blown by the winds of karma into
the twentieth century with all its extravagant abun-
dance and horror—we must have had much in common to start with. Our mirrors, in other words, are
each tilted a little differently yet also focus much of

the light in the same direction, and that light helps make a common human world for us.

CONTINUAL EVOLUTION

At the same time, that world is not holding still. We have already seen that on the level of manifestation appearances are continually changing, as freely and easily as light and shadow. *The Secret Doctrine* reminds us that "Nothing on earth has real duration, for nothing remains without change—or the same— for the billionth part of a second" (I:110/I:37). Yet these changes are not random or purposeless, for they are all under Necessity, under the One Law which runs through all that is.

As background for understanding the meaning of universal evolution, let us again look at the three fundamental propositions which *The Secret Doctrine* uses as openers:

"An Omnipresent, Eternal, Boundless and Immutable PRINCIPLE on which all speculation is impossible, since it transcends the power of human conception...beyond the range and reach of thought." We have already pointed to this Reality and identified it—insofar as one can—with the Unknown Root from which both consciousness and matter stem. It can also be identified as Absolute Consciousness, but this should not be confused with the active consciousness that is in interplay with matter to form the world as we know it.

"The Eternity of the Universe *in toto* as a boundless plane; periodically the playground of numberless Universes incessantly manifesting and disappearing, called the manifesting stars, and the sparks of Eternity. The Eternity of the Pilgrim—the Monad or immortal principle in each individual—is like a wink of the Eye of Self-Existence. The appearance and disappearance of Worlds is like a regular tidal ebb of flux and reflux."

This is the manifesting universe of consciousness and matter. We ought not to proceed without pointing out that this mind-boggling picture of the ultimate universe as a "boundless plane" within which innumerable particular universes blink on and off like lights, in accordance with firm laws of periodicity, is as suggestive of current cosmology as the nineteenth-century *Secret Doctrine* is of current holographic views of consciousness. That the universe began at a single point, called the "Big Bang," and has for twenty billion years expanded outwards has been commonly accepted for some time. Increasingly evidence builds up that the universe contains enough matter to "close" the process at a certain point and commence a contraction, the whole cycle involving some eighty billion years.

However, a mere oscillating universe is not sufficient, since with each cycle entropy would increase and the cycle would be larger and longer: going backward in time one would thus still eventually reach a singular "Big Bang." In other words, an oscillating universe would still not be infinite in duration. The problem of original creation remains.

But in the 1970s and 1980s came a new cosmology presenting a "superspace" out of which countless universes emerge as bubbles triggered by random quantum events, in accordance with the Heisenberg uncertainty principle. Fluctuations in the latent energy of empty space beginning as pointlike disturbances can, under the right circumstances, generate runaway energy that will look like a "Big Bang" from within the nascent universe, eventually to produce galaxies, stars, life, and mind. Again, the tentative nature of scientific hypotheses must be kept in mind, and we must not absolutize this further remarkable convergence between *The Secret Doctrine* and current physical models, but it is suggestive.

For this superspace in which universes continually appear and disappear—as their lights go out in "heat death" or contraction—is like the unknowable but absolute One, the Unknown Root, the boundless plane, which is the sleeping matrix of our and all other universes alluded to in *The Secret Doctrine*. " 'What is that which was, is, and will be, whether there is a Universe or not; whether there be gods or none?' asks the esoteric Senzar Catechism. And the answer made is —'SPACE' " (I:75/I:9). Again:

> It is the ONE LIFE, eternal, yet omnipresent, without beginning or end, yet periodical in its regular manifestations—between which periods reigns the dark mystery of Non-Being; unconscious, yet absolute Consciousness, unrealizable, yet the one self-existing Reality; truly, "a Chaos to the sense, a Kosmos to the reason." Its one absolute attribute, which is Itself, eternal, ceaseless Motion, is called in esoteric parlance the "Great Breath," which is the perpetual motion of the Universe, in the sense of limitless, ever-present Space. That which is motionless cannot be Divine. (I:70/I:2)

Elsewhere *The Secret Doctrine* tells us that what is spoken of in the esoteric sources as Life is what science would speak of simply as Energy. We then have a striking picture of the horizonless primordial superspace, undifferentiated yet alive with energy potential out of which quantum-events, and universes, can spontaneously arise; their periodicity, of which Blavatsky repeatedly speaks, reminds one of the statistical methods one must employ to talk of quantum activity.

The Secret Doctrine also refers to the superspace or ultimate Reality as absolute Consciousness, as we have seen, distinguishing this from the emanated consciousness interacting with various states of matter. Absolute Reality as Absolute Consciousness is something which modern speculative cosmology is not yet ready to speak of scientifically, yet the term should afford no philosophical difficulty. We are not speaking of consciousness of anything in particular, any more than we can speak of energy directed toward particular ends in superspace. That condition can come only with the emergence of actual universes, along with more particularized consciousnesses.

But could consciousness—the ability of the universe to know itself through specific entities within it—appear in a universe if it were not first in the matrix out of which that universe became concretized? More and more, as the holographic model shows, we realize that knowing, the essence of consciousness, is inseparable from the manifest world which is known. Space, time, matter are ways in which we know, and they have no meaning apart from knowledge of them. Looking at the question from another direction (also developed in theosophy), all religions postulate some form of consciousness—God, the gods, the Absolute—prior to creation or manifestation of the phenomenal world.

Cosmologists are also pondering increasingly another remarkable aspect of our particular universe. Not only is it impossible to observe the universe without factoring in how the human observer's mind slices it up; it is also hard to avoid the conclusion that something is very special about our universe to make that human observer possible. A number of features of our system, from the strength of the basic forces to the rate of expansion, happen to be "just right" for the production of suns, heavy elements, and cool planets upon which life can dwell. Had any one of a number of fundamental values been only slightly "off," the existence of even one planet hospitable to life in our universe would have been ruled out.

The convergence of right factors is striking, and we are led to conclude one of the following: a) Some built-in relation obtains between the way a universe is and the existence of minds within it that mirror it: or b) a very large or infinite number of random universes exist, and ours happens to be one that works right for life, which is why we are here: or c) both preceding statements are true. Theosophists would no doubt generally opt for the last statement, pointing out however that if consciousness is as built-in as even our singular universe suggests, it may exist in very different ways or planes in different kinds of universes. Sentient life on planets may be far from the only way in which life, as energy produced by consciousness and matter interacting, manifests itself.

A SPLIT-LEVEL UNIVERSE

Theosophical tradition goes on to relate that consciousness works all the way through the universe as it unfolds outer form from within. A key passage in *The Secret Doctrine* says:

> Parabrahman, the One Reality, the Absolute, is the field of Absolute Consciousness, i.e., that Essence which is out of all relation to conditioned existence, and of which conscious existence is a conditioned symbol. But once we pass in thought

> from this (to us) Absolute Negation, duality super-
> venes in the contrast of Spirit (or Consciousness)
> and Matter, Subject and Object.
>
>   Spirit (or Consciousness) and Matter are, how-
> ever, to be regarded, not as independent realities,
> but as the two symbols or aspects of the Absolute,
> Parabrahman, which constitute the basis of con-
> ditioned Being whether subjective or objective.
> (I:80/I:15)

Here we see articulation of what might be called a
split-level universe, divided between Unconditioned
and Conditioned Reality. This distinction is generally basic to religion, whether put in the language of
sacred and profane, God and world, or Brahman and
Maya. Theosophy presents it in philosophical terms
which converge with scientific cosmology.

Let us start with conditioned reality, since that is
what most of us know most about. We are continually conditioned by space, time, and the finitude of
the human mind. If we are in, say, Chicago or London, we are not also in Cape Town or Katmandu. If
we are living in the twentieth century, we cannot
also be in the ninth with Charlemagne or the twenty-
fifth with Buck Rogers. We cannot ordinarily think
of more than one thing at a time; we remember only a
tiny fragment of what passes our way; most of us
cannot multiply more than simple two-digit numbers
in our heads. Even worse, our thinking is precondi-
tioned by all sorts of desires, fears, and self-images
we carry about. We consciously or unconsciously
think, "I'm a person who always wants this, is afraid
of that, likes this, dislikes that, believes this, disbe-
lieves that," until we've built ourselves a cage as
strong as iron bars from which we dare not stir, and
only through its grill are we able to face other people

or fresh thoughts. All this is of the nature of conditioned reality.

Some may hold that conditioned reality is all there is, or at least all that can be known. Theosophy, like religion, proposes otherwise. In these perspectives, conditioned reality could not exist, or would be incomprehensible, without an opposite. Just as positive charges presuppose negative or matter antimatter, so conditioned reality presupposes Unconditioned Reality as its opposite and matrix. In it, all time and place are one, all thought and energy are unlimited. It is pure space and pure consciousness.

Out of this field with the first bubble-universe come Spirit or Consciousness and Matter interacting. From their intermingling come the concrete forms of the universe, including ourselves. Both aspects of the universe derive from the ultimate field, the Unknown Root or Absolute Consciousness or Unconditioned Reality. From its unconditioned consciousness comes spirit, from its unconditioned motion or energy comes matter (which, as we know from physics, is simply particular patterns of energy). But now they interact to create a field of energy which makes conditioned consciousness as we know it, and conditioned consciousness in turn makes (or rather selects for itself from out of the universal hologram) the appearance of particular configurations of matter which accord with its state.

We should make special note of the use of the word *symbol* in the above passage from Blavatsky, as it speaks of conscious existence as a "conditioned symbol" and of spirit and matter as "two symbols" of the Absolute. *Symbol* is a very important word in the world's religious and spiritual traditions. The word literally means in Greek "falls with," suggesting something which bears with it more than itself. The theologian Paul Tillich has spoken of symbols as participating in that which they symbolize. To interact with a symbol, in other words, is to interact with more than the thing itself; it also brings one in touch with another reality.

Here let us distinguish between sign and symbol. A sign, like one telling how many miles it is to the next town, merely conveys a message, or so it would to most people. The sign does not "participate" in those miles. But if the driver were a person returning after many years absence to the town in which he had grown up, seeing that sign might have an impact far beyond just the factual information of how many miles he still had to go. It might begin to evoke the sights, the sounds, even the smells of long ago, till he was inwardly participating in what the name of that town meant. Likewise, for a lover the picture of the beloved is more than just a casual reminder of someone, and for a believer the cross on a church or the star and crescent on a mosque are more than just indicators of what sort of building it is; they may call up a warm feeling of faith and a sense of the divine presence they symbolize.

When our conscious existence, and spirit and matter themselves, are spoken of as *symbols* of unconditioned reality, this is an important statement. It tells us that our own awareness and our own physical being—as well as all that we see around us of matter shaped by its intricate interaction with spirit—enable us to participate in Ultimate Reality. We participate in it through these symbols as much as we participate in our own reality. We would know that we are and all we see is Ultimate Reality in disguise, unlimited Being and Bliss, if we could break its code. One is reminded of those Zen teachers who tell us that the Buddha-nature is the hedge at the back of the garden, and enlightenment is to be found in washing dishes after one has eaten. In theosophy, for all the elaborate-seeming chains of descent between the original Unconditioned Reality and where we are at now, we must never forget that they are not chains in our kind of space and time, and Unconditioned Reality is never far away—it is here now, in, with, and under conditioned reality.

In format, most of *The Secret Doctrine* is commentary on an esoteric text called the "Stanzas of Dzyan," which describes in strange, colorful, and mythical language these processes of the emergence of a universe bearing consciousness and matter. Those more accustomed to the expressions of contemporary science may find passages such as the following at first bizarre:

> The last vibrations of the Seventh Eternity thrilled through Infinitude. The Mother swelled expanding from *within without* like the bud of the lotus. The vibration swept along touching with its swift wing simultaneously the whole universe, and the germ that dwelleth in Darkness, the Darkness that breathes [moves] over the slumbering waters of life. Darkness radiated Light, and light dropped one solitary Ray into the Waters of Mother Space. The ray fructified [recalled to life] the 'Eternal Virgin Egg' (I:102/I:28).

Could this not be considered a metaphor in picture language of the quantum event (quanta are units of light) which engendered a universe? We go on to read of the egg producing a father and mother who in turn bear a radiant child: spirit, matter, and the new individualizing consciousness in all its wonder and terror.

The language of *The Secret Doctrine*, as of theosophy generally, is no more than "pointer" language, able to inspire thoughts in the course of one's jnana yoga that ultimately must be negated for deeper portrayals in the mind—and these too are not final. The end of probing into ultimate mysteries is never reached. Yet this language performs a wonderful function, like that of the myth and ritual of all religion.

The borderline between conditioned and Unconditioned Reality is far from hermetically sealed. It is replete with doors and windows through which messages are passed and people come and go. These doors and windows are the symbols and stock-in-trade of religion; they are its doctrines, rites, institutions, arts, and practices such as prayer and meditation. Their great value is that they put Unconditioned Reality in humanly significant form. They color and shape its white light, like a stained glass window, into teachers, saviors, healing rites, and holy assemblies. As doorways, they offer specific entrances to the Other Side, according to the particular spiritual tradition: this form of prayer, that kind of meditation or faith. By shaping Unconditioned Reality into particular forms, they make it speak the language of our world in which everything comes particularized: people, places, times, practices, concepts. Unconditioned Reality then becomes the burden of a special saving person, a holy place or time, a sacred rite, an ultimately true idea. By giving Unconditioned Reality a human face, the borderline doors and windows make it part of our world—as it must be, since it undergirds it.

As we have seen, theosophy recognizes the importance of images and ideas in leading us on the path of jnana yoga to Ultimate Reality, while also indicating that they must eventually be transcended. *The Secret Doctrine*, when it uses the language of womb and germ, of father, mother, and child, shows the human significance of the time of origins. And why shouldn't it? That moment in the unimaginable deeps of time is intertwined with our lives today.

What we are now was started then, when a flash of light awakened the energy-particle that became the great household which is our universe. Male and female, parent and child may not have become actualized in present human form until the peopling of our world, but they were latent even then, expressed in the creative polarization of Spirit and Matter. To use mythical language and speak of the latent in terms of the realized forms does no violence to truth for the wise, but only augments truth. It shows profound analogies and interconnections throughout the living universal system. For the fruit is encoded in the flower and the flower in the seed.

In particular, in speaking as she does of principles which can be spoken of as male and female occurring all the way through the universal evolution, Blavatsky presents a picture which undoubtedly will be more appealing to many than that of those religious systems that use almost exclusively the language of one sex for the divine.

ON PILGRIMAGE

The third of the Three Fundamental Propositions of *The Secret Doctrine* is: "The fundamental identity of all Souls with the Universal Oversoul, the latter being itself an aspect of the Unknown Root; and the obligatory pilgrimage for every Soul—a spark of the former—through the Cycle of incarnation, or Necessity, in accordance with cyclic and karmic law, during the whole term."

Evolution from the lowest to the highest, through all the kingdoms of nature, is incumbent on each Pilgrim. Every such soul, we are told, must have "passed through every elemental form of the phenomenal world of that Manvatara" (or manifest universe), and "acquired individuality, first by natural impulse, and then by self-induced and self-devised efforts, checked by its Karma, thus ascending through all the degrees of intelligence, from the lowest to the highest Manas [Mind], from mineral and plant, up to the holiest Archangel," before it has fulfilled its obligation and become entirely free.

These individual entities are called Souls, Monads, or Pilgrims. They are precipitated out of the primordial interaction of Spirit and Matter and are necessarily finite. For when spirit conjoins with matter, it is constricted by the latter's existence as energy subject to natural law. Matter is subject to attraction and repulsion, change and decay. Matter itself constantly seeks elusive rest in lower levels of expression, as in the slowing of a pendulum or the cooling of red-hot iron or the eventual death of all organisms. Conversely, spirit seeks fuller and fuller expression. When matter is joined to spirit, as it always is, it is energized by tension between matter's inertia and spirit's yearning for its true home in ultimate unconditioned Reality. Striving to swim against the conditioned world's current of decay, spirit creates that conditioned reality as it struggles to transcend it. Along the way it expresses itself through manifold forms, from mineral through plant and animal to human and god, on its return with its material envelopes to its eternal home.

We must remind ourselves again that in so putting it we speak the language of one level of jnana yoga. As the same passage of *The Secret Doctrine* states, in a deeper sense these "permutations, psychic, spiritual and physical, on the plane of manifestation and form" are "mayavic," "no better than an evanescent illusion of our senses." Yet as important as such realizations are, it is also true that one can ordinarily expect no faster progress on the road toward ultimate wisdom than what accords with the way one *really* thinks of oneself, not just the way one theoretically philosophizes.

If the way we live most of life really says we are separate individual selves with our own wants and virtues and beliefs and fears, then the path of growth will first be toward more virtue and purer belief, with fewer self-centered wants and fears. Not a few aspirants have been set far back by attempting to plunge into deep levels of realization when they were ready for only the merest beginning glimmer to be patiently cultivated. If one who is still essentially ego-bound endeavors to treat the rest of the world as only illusion, the result will be no more than solipsist madness, sinking deeper and deeper into a black hole of egocentricity.

For the long pilgrimage is governed, as the passage just quoted tells us, by two "checks": cycles and karma, the cause-and-effect on all levels of thought and deed to which we have already referred. These inexorable laws keep us, despite the deep eagerness of spirit for home and matter for rest, from travelling faster than the road allows. While one who gets his vehicle in superb operating condition can indeed make excellent headway, one is nonetheless always traveling with a larger company and can never leave unfinished business along the way.

Traveling with a larger company bespeaks cycles. No concept is more basic to theosophy than that the phenomena of the universe follow periodicity, or cycles large and small. Just as there is day and night, so is there the coming and going of universes, systems, worlds, and races. These manifestations, as we shall see later, occur successively on various "planes" of matter from the very subtlest to physical substance as we know it. Each manifestation provides unique opportunities for the accumulation of diverse experience which is essential for the maturation of the Pilgrim. In large part, souls linked by affinity and comparable stages of growth pass from world to world in companies. Some may go to the head of their grouping or even transcend it altogether, while others may lag behind, but that is exceptional. In general it is the cycles which "program" the experiences needed for normal growth, and one's development is broadly governed by their stately pace. (In the deeper sense, of course, it is partly the other way around—the stage of the development of souls helps shape the worlds in which their level of growth can be expressed.)

Karma is a Sanskrit word whose fundamental meaning is "action" or "movement" and what results from it. Cause and effect are essential to all activity; nothing in the physical world moves without sufficient cause. Further, all activity exerts energy on whatever it impacts, which rebounds back on it from the force of the impact. Theosophy, like the Eastern religious traditions from which the concept of karma derives, perceives that a comparable pattern of cause and effect obtains on the moral and spiritual planes as well. Our thoughts, words, and deeds produce appropriate results in this life or a life to come: good results in blessing; ill produces bane.

Karma and reincarnation are clearly related concepts. Reincarnation is the idea that our essential being, the consciousness-principle called the monad or Pilgrim, passes from one body to another after physical death (and through an intermediate state, the Devachan). Rebirth, along with karma, expresses the kinetic, cause-and-effect principle operative on all levels, physical and moral. This principle says that a cause set in motion on any level cannot fade until it has produced an appropriate effect. A stone cast into a pond will produce ripples that persist until their energy is exhausted or until they reach the shore. A human lifetime is not finished with physical death because it has also set in motion, through all its thoughts, words, deeds, moral and spiritual energies which must be worked out. Since they were set in motion in a human life, they can be worked out only in another life of equal consequence.

The working out will be connected to the basic purpose of the monad's incarnation. For those who have reached the path of return to the One, this will mean expanding awareness and power through negation of egocentricity in compassion and service. That is, our energies are to be worked out through more and more profound realization of Oneness and the interaction of all being, for compassion and service are simply the ethical expression of Unity, awareness of the illusive nature of all that seems to separate and differentiate the entities of this spirit/matter universe.

Therefore, to put it succinctly, all we do in the way of selfless compassion and service will bring as its logical consequence enhanced *experience* of the basic Oneness through enhanced awareness and power—even eventual rebirth as one with the calling of a great saint or great soul. Here is at work the paradoxial but crucial truth inculcated by all spiritual masters, that he who gives up his life for the sake of higher things will find it, and find it a hundredfold.

The person who lives on the basis of the false premise that the separate individual self is absolute, and that one makes one's way by asserting and aggrandizing it over all else that lives, will receive the consequences of living in such a world of strife and bitterness. For finally we *do* live in the sort of world in which we believe. One who is fearful will find in this arena of life much to fear; one who loves, much to love. Much truth resides in the old saying that, "He who lives by the sword will die by the sword," as history exemplifies time and time again. Karma tells us that the person of violence, lust, or hate attracts not only retribution but also learning, in the form of knowing from the other side what it is like to live in a realm so made. The murderer may undergo the horror of sudden brutal death, the slaver the degradation of being a slave. Such learning may in time create an inner emptiness able to open one to the realization of Oneness in its place.

This is not to say we are entitled to look on the suffering of anyone with indifference on the grounds that, because of karma, it is "deserved." We who do not know all root causes and ends have no right to pass such judgments. We must not forget that karmic causes from other lives are generally not consciously known. Only on a deep level where it may do little to alleviate immediate suffering, is the work of karma being done. Most important by far, our own imperative in such a cosmos is always the labor of compassion and service regardless of the reasons for the suffering. If one is opened to a broader realization through suffering the consequences of egocentricity, it is very likely to be through the ministrations of one who was compassionate in that very moment of anguish, who thereby showed the greatness of love and the Oneness it proclaims. Karma is not determinism; our own input through wisdom and compassion has an effect here and hereafter.

So it is that through cycles and the cause-and-effect of karma that we, and all other bearers of consciousness in this universe of spirit and matter interfused, find our way back from the primal precipitating-out of individualization to ultimate return. But the return is not to the original undifferentiated Unknown Root but to a godlike clarity which combines the former unconditioned state with all enhancement of thought won through the long pilgrimage. Unimaginable stages may lie even beyond that in endless universes to come. But for us in midpassage, it is enough to know that progress can be made through wisdom and compassion and that there are those ahead of us who, out of their own much greater wisdom and compassion, can extend a helping hand. However, we must have the perspicuity to hear them or find them, for being deeper into Oneness they are, to our still half-blind eyes, mysterious and hard to discover.

ANCIENT WISDOM

Such wisdom as this, theosophy emphasizes, is the heritage of all humankind, not just of a single sect or people.

The principle of Oneness applies to human wisdom just as it does to the universe as a whole. (This is another application of the basic theosophical law of analogy, or "as above, so below.") Just as the Oneness of the universe is more fundamental than its diversity, so what is most widespread and most expresses unity among the spiritual and philosophical traditions of the Earth is most true in the eyes of theosophists.

To be sure, underlying unities may not always be readily apparent. The universe is one, yet it also displays an astounding richness of diversity in its concrete manifestation. This is part of its power. The splendid manifoldness awakens in us that sense of wonder which is the beginning of wisdom, though the end of wisdom may be a profound awareness of the One. Similarly, the rich panorama of the world's religions and philosophies should be regarded by the seeker as more than a mere distraction. It provides opportunities on the human plane for awakening wonder, for marvelous aesthetic appreciation, above all for deep inner understanding of another's culture and society. All this is excellent turf for exercises in jnana yoga aimed at "intuiting the essences" behind religion's countless forms, and in those essences, rightly divined, unities will be found.

What are these unities? There are several of special importance for the theosophical worldview.

Oneness. Virtually all religions posit a single unifying source of Reality: God, Brahman, the Tao, the Dharmakaya of Mahayana Buddhism. Whether a definite *moment* of creation is affirmed or whether the generation of the world is an eternal or cyclical process is a matter of relative truth; the crucial point is that the universe of multiplicity is always viewed as contingent upon the One. Even most polytheistic systems embody a fundamental principle of unity which shows that the many gods ultimately work in harmony, for example, the "high god" and the sense of Nature of primitives, the *ma'at* principle and the sovereignty of Amon in ancient Egypt.

Spiritual Energy. Further, religions tend to affirm that the One acts in the world through a power or "substance" which, though it may ultimately be simply the indivisible divine presence, appears to humans as a special, fluid kind of energy, such as God's

grace or Holy Spirit in Christianity, *shakti* (or maya
in the sense of divine power over appearances) in
Hinduism, or *baraka* or the sacred energy surround-
ing saints in mystical Islam.

A central theme of *Isis Unveiled*, Helena Blavatsky's first major work, is the universal availability
of a rarefied energy known to the wise of all
lands by which seeming magic can be done; it is not,
however, magic strictly speaking for it employs little-
known yet natural laws. This energy, in fact, is spirit,
which as we have seen has been produced from the
One together with matter since the beginning of our
universe and which, in interaction with matter, precipitates individualized consciousnesses. The operation of consciousness is actually "magical" in no different sense from the illusions of magicians or the
psychokinesis of adepts, for it causes actions, such as
the movement of the body, without evident material
cause. Yet without the energizing presence of spirit
to give emotion and the matter of the brain subjective
awareness, they would be just automata. This spirit,
we are told in *Isis Unveiled*, can also be wielded as a
"detached" power transcending ordinary nature by
those who know its secrets.

Cycles. If a ruling theme of *Isis Unveiled* is
"magic," so one of *The Secret Doctrine* is the fundamentally cyclical nature of reality. The cycles of nature are fairly obvious; religions, like theosophy, tend
to perceive tides in the affairs of men as well. Hinduism and Buddhism, like Platonism in the West, see
the world made and unmade over and over, without
beginning or end, through immense periods of time;
by these sources Helena Blavatsky was most directly
influenced.

The Western monotheistic religions—Judaism,
Christianity, and Islam—generally attribute a defi-

nite point of creation ex *nihilo* to the present world
and see its wrapping up at some definite future
point. But they also perceive in history definite
"ages" or "dispensations" of great spiritual significance: in the case of Christianity, those governed by
God's "covenants" with Adam, Noah, Abraham,
Moses and the Law, and by Christ with his atoning
death. In a real sense, theosophy affirms the inner
meaning of both of these perspectives. It presents the
eternal cyclical outlook of the East, while saying with
the Western faiths that history has meaning, that the
cycles are not just identical but build on each other,
so that successive human eras, like successive
worlds and universes, are evolving and in the long
view getting better.

Initiations. Allusion has been made to the widespread motif of initiation, as a mystery of death-and-
rebirth or self-transformation in a religious context.
In virtually all faiths, some definite rite of passage—
inner, outer, or both—assists the believer to transit
the major stages of life, from birth through puberty
and adulthood through death. Initiation may also
bring one across the threshold of a special vocation,
such as that of shaman or priest, or mark the great
turnings of one's inward progress toward holiness
and liberation.

In primitive religion, one thinks of the initiations
of young men, which may involve seclusion, circum-
cision, and the "vision quest"; and of the shaman's
call, with its preliminary "madness," its deathlike ordeal which might include "taking out" one's bones
and counting them, its final bestowal of marvelous
flight, power over spirits, and knowledge of the paths
taken by the dead. In Christianity, initiation encompasses baptism, the ordination of priests and minis-
ters (after, presumably, an inward call), and on a

deeper plane transitions such as the "baptism of the
Spirit" of Pentecostalists and the "dark night of the
soul" of St John of the Cross.

The theosophical tradition accepts the universal
principle of initiation, and acknowledges the witness
given it by the rites of passage of all faiths, as well as
by Masonic and comparable lodges. In its own lore,
however, it is inward initiations, given by the generally invisible Masters or Adepts, which figure most
prominently.

Advanced Spiritual Teachers. The belief in "Masters" is sometimes represented as a rather bizarre notion of theosophists, but in fact it is virtually as universal as any of the other ideas presented here from
the world's religions. Almost all faiths hold in some
form to the assertion that some human beings, by
dint of extraordinary spiritual practice or divine
grace, have acquired wisdom and power far beyond
the ordinary. Whether in this life or some other plane
these beings exercise what seems to us a semidivine
calling to guide and protect struggling humanity. But
the significant point is that these sublime beings
were once humans, as frail and fallible as we. They
have risen to the heights to which we also can and
(according to theosophy) eventually will ascend.
These are the saints of Christianity, especially in
Catholic and Orthodox devotion, and of mystical
Islam; the rishis (sages) and jivanmuktas (God-realized persons) of Hinduism; the Buddhas and bodhisattvas of Buddhism; the immortals of Taoism.

Theosophy characteristically accepts the general
picture of beneficent advanced souls offered by the
world's faiths, but universalizes this idea to say in effect that all the saints of all religions are real. Far
from being in competition with each other, as parti-
san zealots might claim, they form an assembly to

guard and guide humankind. Much theosophical literature insists that many Masters, despite their remarkable powers, are in human bodies and dwell ordinarily in some out-of-the-way part of the earth. In addition to the well-known saints and seers of all religions, theosophy acknowledges a few others, such as the Masters Morya and Kuthumi, who were particularly close to Helena Blavatsky and the other founders of the Theosophical Society. Some theosophical literature, most impressively C.W. Leadbeater's *The Masters and the Path*, offers fascinating and detailed accounts of the Masters and their functions. Today many theosophists would prefer to speak only with reserve about such matters, as we shall see later.

Certain general ideas about the Masters, however, seem important to a theosophical worldview. One is that though from many times and places they form a great Brotherhood united in service, into which anyone who is prepared can be inwardly initiated. The second is that they form a heirarchy, an "Inner Government of the World." Beginning with those on the lower reaches of this *cursus honorum*, it extends beyond our world to unimaginably exalted heirarchies of solar systems, constellations, galaxies, and universes. The idea is not to give oneself over unduly to idle speculation on such things, but to grasp the spiritually salutary truth that one can "move up," for the way is open and the heights unlimited.

Despite the fact that the traditional writing seems to emphasize Masters who appear in masculine guise, authors like Leadbeater also stress that the heirarchy has a feminine side. There is a World Mother, who incarnated as the Virgin Mary, and the higher entities embrace both masculine and feminine powers, who, like the universe itself, are beyond gender as we know it.

Finally, we note that the Masters are accessible to sincere and qualified seekers. Many theosophical stories indicate commerce with them. The old saying, "When the student is ready, the Master appears," has been accepted (and found true) by many theosophists. Those who wish to help in the great work of promoting the beauty and unity of earth, along with the well-being of all its myriad souls, will not find themselves alone—though a season of seeming loneliness may be a part of their initiatory ordeal.

Theosophy, then, is a tradition whose wisdom penetrates vast cosmological reaches of space and time and immense eras of human history. It perceives great cycles in their turning and the working out of cause-and-effect. It sees also, throughout the human world, a wisdom tradition by which our experiences can be interpreted in the widest possible context. We must now turn to the specifics of that tradition.

2
Universes, Solar Systems, Worlds

We have seen that universes begin as "bubbles" in the "boundless plane" of superspace. According to recent scientific estimates, our particular universe is some 20 billion years old and contains an incredible 100 billion galaxies—twenty for every man, woman, and child on earth—each swarming with stars and probably worlds in numbers beyond imagining.

Nor is that all. Cosmologists are now beginning to think seriously of our universe, with all its oceanic immensities and shoals of suns, as after all just our own particular hometown, only one of many—perhaps an infinite number—of other universes. They sparkle throughout a superspace which is, to return to the words of Helena Blavatsky, "the playground of numberless Universes incessantly manifesting and disappearing," like "sparks of Eternity."

But why do these universes appear? Why does the Unknown Root set aside its anonymity sufficiently to come veiled as stars and worlds? Neither cosmology nor theosophy can do more than hint at an answer, so far above the normal range of human thought is a question like this. Theosophy can supplement science, though, when it postulates consciousness as present right from the beginning along with matter.

The way in which consciousness works helps us to understand why there are universes. Consciousness wants to experience awareness, to know. The moment we wake up in the morning we become aware —of the bedroom, the clock, the birds outside the window. Consciousness needs to set part of itself outside itself, so to speak, so that there can be knower and known, subject and object. The universe, then, is a mirror in which the Absolute—God, if you wish—knows itself.

If, as *The Secret Doctrine* says, universes are infinite in number, "numberless," then in unimaginable depths of space and time all possible worlds would exist. Every possible variation in the arrangements of atoms and molecules and all else would ultimately come to pass; all the worlds of human fantasy, and all possible variations in history and in the course of each life, would somewhere have reality, so it would seem.

All we can be sure of, though, from the theosophical perspective, is that in all worlds and universes the path back to the One is open, for the One is the underlying reality beneath the infinite variations. While a flowering tree may obscure its root, it does not lose the inward paths to that root through which it seeks nourishment. As on the one hand the Unknown Root expresses its unconditioned Reality in the form of infinite Oneness, so on the other hand in manifestation it may express the same as infinite multiplicity.

The *Bhagavad-Gita,* an ancient Hindu text highly valued by many theosophists, suggests as much when, in the stupendous theophany of Krishna (the

One) appearing to Arjuna (the seeker) in visible form, it makes that supreme God reveal himself "infinite of arms, eyes, mouths, and bellies—. . . See, and find no end, midst, or beginning." But whether or not the boundless plane of appearing and disappearing universes is actually infinite multiplicity we cannot know, at least by any means conceivable at present. *The Secret Doctrine* speaks of a "Ring-Pass-Not" around our system, which we could perhaps expand to mean the space-time continuum of our particular universe.

Amid such speculation, we must never forget that all we *really* need to know is the next step on our own path. Yet occasionally a high pass on any trail brings into sight imposing vistas—range after range of mountain peaks, deep valleys, and lush meadows. The panorama thrills us with the awesome dimensions of the journey, with the greatness of whence we have come and the splendor of where we are going. While speculation about remote origins and destinies in the theosophical style may get out of hand, judicious attention to it can indeed open up the magnificent visions we need to encourage us through the heat and dust of our daily passages. So let us now raise our sights to the high terrain.

We have already seen that the One Reality, "the field of Absolute Consciousness," Unconditioned Reality, primordially expresses itself as spirit (or consciousness in potentially finite form) and matter, which "are, however, to be regarded, not as independent realities, but as two symbols, or aspects of the Absolute, Parabrahman, which constitute the basis of conditioned Being whether subjective or objective" (*The Secret Doctrine* I:80/I:15).

Out of these two come the universes and worlds. Their interplay creates a universe because matter gives spirit specific content, and spirit lends matter shape as it expresses the nature of specific discrete consciousness. If a mind "wants"—that is, requires at its particular level—a world of mental or solid substance, harsh or beautiful, fearsome or loving, then through the interaction of spirit and matter such a world and that mind are drawn to each other.

It must be emphasized that spirit and matter are conjoined at every point. Sometimes spirit predominates as in humans and higher beings. Sometimes matter predominates as in minerals. Both matter and spirit can be respectively tenuous or dense, but both are always there.

The evolution of the universe should be thought of as bringing what is latent into form. We shall soon be talking about series of worlds, but these should not necessarily be considered developments in time as we know it. We have already reviewed the subjective nature of time described in *The Secret Doctrine*. These series are stages of the emergence of spirit and matter into our space-time continuum. Or to look at it from another side, our minds bring consciousness-realities into focus by attuning them to our style of space, time, and matter.

We make a universe that suits the way we want to see things. If, as do most people at our present stage, we essentially see ourselves as a separate consciousness walking around in a detached body, we sharpen the focus until the demarcation between consciousness and matter becomes very clear. We thus create for ourselves the individual consciousness with all its hopes and fears.

INVOLUTION AND EVOLUTION

Theosophy presents the career of a universe and its life in terms of involution and evolution, two very important concepts. Involution is the process of consciousness/spirit getting more and more deeply involved, as energy or life, in its eternal companion, matter. This is an outward-bound journey of exploration and learning for the Pilgrim. In the process, matter itself takes on denser and denser forms, as though to explore its own potential in conjunction with spirit, or better, to explore more fully what the pair can do together.

In the adventure, the Life-Pilgrim at once enables the Absolute to know itself through objectification and loses itself, almost inevitably at first, in the labyrinths of time and space. Spirit and matter conjoined hold up the mirror of space and time to the face of God and forget themselves in the glitter. They chase each other down halls of light, finally ending together in a world such as ours. Here matter is as solid as it can get, and spirit seems as other-than-matter as it can be; the focus of demarcation is turned very sharply.

In a world like ours, spirit and matter indeed often appear at odds with each other. But it is important to realize they are inseparable, they both came from the One, and are both symbols of it. Their interplay is no more than a game. But in our sphere the game is at a high pitch, and the distinction between the two players may seem as marked as between white and black in chess. During play, one side can advance far into the territory of the other, block the other's moves, or even remove an opposing piece from the board. But when the game is over, black and white go together into the shadowy box, side by side and still.

An hour eventually comes, in accordance with immense cycles, when the denizens of such a world have gone "out" as far as one can, and the long rapture of return to the One commences. Actually this homeward journey began on our planet with the coming of life, for the slow evolution of vitality from mineral through plant and animal and human is a prelude to spirit becoming freer and the matter joined with it more tenuous. But the return has only begun. For most humans, still very much enmeshed in matter as a separating experience, it is not yet conscious.

Yet eventually, impelled by long tides set very deep in the channels of mind, we realize we are moving, and the focus of our perception of how spirit, matter, and the One interact changes. This is the start of conscious evolution, the great return to Unity, which in due course will take us out of worlds of "dense" matter altogether.

We may already have felt hints of the change. Consider how real/unreal this world we have colonized can seem. Can't you remember hours when its soil and throbbing life were incredibly real and other times when they seem to fade just a little, like a reverie when the doorbell rings? And haven't there been moments when you sensed something unnamed but thicker than the world of separate appearances flow in you, making that world seem thin and filmy? For an instant, the way we'd gotten used to things went out of focus.

The process of sharpening and then defusing the focus on dense matter in its conjunction with spirit, then, is the process of involution and evolution: the descent of the Pilgrim, life-consciousness, into a world like ours and then back out of it. It is a great chain which presupposes that life-consciousness has been there with matter from the outset of the universe (though at first it was very tenuous "abstract" matter such as space, time, and energy). Such a universe has never been, and could never be, without life and consciousness—though consciousness also begins in nonconcretized form. Individualized mind, thinly filmed in matter, was first only implicit and latent, awaiting vehicles of individuation. But the vehicles would never pull up to the cosmic doors were someone not waiting to utilize them.

At certain points the development of spirit and matter may appear to pursue relatively separate tracks. "Solid" material worlds may be only under preparation, while the consciousnesses which will inhabit them—now spirit with only thin films of matter—is undergoing very different tailoring in realms which though material, are not yet solid. Still the two sides go together, and according to *The Secret Doctrine* are linked by the mysterious force that binds all things together, which facilitates their interaction. To an omniscient eye the two would not really be very far apart—they need and shape each other, and both are but symbols of the One.

The Three Outpourings

Now we must look more exactly at the teachings of theosophy on the making of this consciousness-and-matter universe of ours. It *starts* as the awakening of latent consciousness and energy within the One in the form of self-expression or objectification, which from another point of view is involution.

This expression or energizing takes form as three waves surging through the nascent cosmos. They are called *logoi*, plural of the Greek *logos*. Literally *logos* means "word," not too inaccurate a rendering if you think of a word as a form of expression. But in philosophy *logos* has much broader connotations: principle, energy, form. It is the term used at the beginning of St John's Gospel: "In the beginning was the

Word [Logos], and the Word was with God, and the Word was God."

Just as Christians believe that there are three Persons—Father, Son, and Holy Spirit—in the one God, distinct yet also profoundly one, so the theosophical tradition speaks of the three *logoi* (or if you prefer three aspects of one *Logos* or divine manifestation), streaming out from the unmanifest One as divine creative principles and energies. Together these three are like God in the active, Creator sense familiar to most Christians, or the Saguna Brahman, Brahman or God "with attributes," of Vedanta Hinduism —God manifest outward to the world in vigorous personal form.

This divine Trinity of three *logoi* or three aspects of the *Logos* goes by different names. In theosophical literature the three streams are often called Atma, Buddhi, and Manas—Essence (Atma) and Intellect (Buddhi), the familiar matter and spirit in their most transcendent aspects, activated into manifestation as Manas (mind). Sometimes the three are also spoken of as Will, Wisdom, and Activity.

I would like to refer as well to a set of terms occasionally mentioned in the writings of Helena Blavatsky and known to many students of traditional wisdom East and West. These are the three qualities of God or Brahman in Vedanta philosophy: *Sat, Chit,* and *Ananda,* or Being, Consciousness, and Bliss. These are far from inconsistent with the other sets, for surely the highest expression of Will is to Be, and of Being is Matter (in its high sense as energy and extension, or space-time) or Essence (Atma), while Consciousness, Intellect, Spirit, and Wisdom are closely related, and the highest quality of manifested Mind is to experience Bliss.

These are all qualities from which the Unknown outpours universes. The nature of its being is to display infinite existence, of its consciousness to know itself, and of its bliss to dance out worlds in that divine play the Hindus call *lila*.

Theosophy also emphasizes that this same triune Logos is reflected throughout the universe, wherever there is a "local" center of creativity recapitulating the cosmic. Such a center is the heart of the Solar Logos which has been symbolized as ruling our solar system like a divine regent enthroned in the golden palaces of the Sun. This logoic essence is also enthroned in each of us as the divine spark, for we humans are miniatures or microcosms of God, being subcreators.

That of God within us is our true and ultimate nature, our legacy from the glory which is our true home. Despite all that is passing away in our lives, if we look within we know that we have a core of being which simply *is*, which we realize is beyond, or beneath, all vicissitudes. That knowledge in itself guarantees that we have a capacity, despite the mightiness of our delusions, for authentic wisdom which, as ancient scriptures say, is able to separate the real from the unreal. In the depths of our being, beneath the layers of business and buzzing confusion, is an ocean of creativity, wisdom, and joy which we can sometimes tap. In its further reaches this ocean flows into the endless sea of cosmic being.

These three aspects of the One comprise the "core" of creation out of which the rest precipitates in the form of "worlds" in four increasingly dense states of matter. This involutionary series culminates in a world of the sort of matter—solid, liquid, gas, plus "etheric" (to be defined later)—that we know.

This makes seven states in all: the three of the Trinity, plus four refinements of matter through which the universe as an interplay of consciousness and matter is enacted.

In exactly the same way, a human being as a microcosm consists of seven "bodies"—the triune core or divine spark within composed of transcendent essence, consciousness, and mind or bliss, plus the four increasingly dense "sheaths" through which that divine life is expressed in our separate individualized form. These four sheaths parallel the four planes emanating from the Trinity on which worlds are actualized and through which the Pilgrim journeys. We will discuss these planes a little farther on.

First, however, it is important to emphasize that, while in a discussion like this it is difficult to avoid terms like above, below, planes, sheaths, such terms are strictly metaphorical. The planes and worlds interpenetrate one another. They are essentially states of consciousness and matter which can coexist in the same space. What we really mean when we speak of one as "above" or "within" another is ontological priority: that the "lower" or "outer" depends on the former and is in some way fashioned by it.

THE OUTFLOWINGS

Let us return then to the story of the creation of our universe. Technically, *The Secret Doctrine* is largely about the emergence of our solar system, but it is fair to assume this parallels the universal process. We will deal with our local system and Earth specifically, when we come to the case of separate worlds, assuming something stupendous but parallel happens in the case of other stars, galaxies, and the universe as a whole as it proceeds from origin to dense material expression.

The first great outflow or *logos* of divine creative energy, then, is Atma—Sat, essence or being itself. It thus represents the impersonal, sheer being-nature of Ultimate Reality, and as such can be thought of as matter in its most transcendent form as energized space. As the highest plane of which we can have any comprehension whatsoever, it is sometimes referred to in theosophy as the divine "breath" or as Adi, the supreme Source. This outflow might be thought of as the awakening. It energizes the "bubble" of the potential universe to shape its amphitheatre of space and time. As Einstein has taught us, matter is energy (as also is consciousness). With the energizing of the universal field, matter is ready to take shape in interplay with consciousness.

The second *logos* or outflow is spoken of in *The Secret Doctrine* as "Spirit-Matter," for here that fundamental interplay commences. It is the beginning of what might be called "organized energy," life, or at least energy ultimately continuous with life-forms as we know them. As we have seen, what esotericists speak of as life, science would simply call energy. Here is the actual beginning of it all. Organization means process, and process depends upon dualities —forces in interaction. It would not be strictly correct to say that the second *logos* is, or adds, consciousness, for consciousness is inseparable from matter from the first, and if the first *logos* is matter in some supremely elevated form, then consciousness is also there. But now the two begin their interaction and so inaugurate the process of becoming spirit and matter as we can know or imagine them. By the same token, knowledge or awareness comes into manifestation.

This stage climaxes with the third *logos* or outflow, the coming of *manas*, mind, expressed in bliss and activity. Now appear the monads or pilgrims, individualized centers of consciousness. They are the product of matter and spirit in interaction to create individuation as a result of objectification, consciousness's awareness of the distinction between knower and known as it interacts with the extension in space and time inherent in matter.

Ultimately a separate consciousness starts as a separate joy, and it is in the exalted activity or play of spirit-matter stemming from its gift of objectified knowledge that separate selfhood arises. To know is to be distinct from as well as (in another sense) conjoined with, and a sense of distinctness begins with a shout of joy, the cry of a new birth. So it is that as the third wave passes over the field of creation, countless monads awaken in joy and commence their long pilgrimage through the manifold realms of existence.

Note that the three *logoi* or outflows bear a rough resemblance to the three entities—Father Light, Mother Space, and the child as individualized consciousness—of the "myth" cited in Chapter I. The *logoi* convey in the tongue of Greek philosophy what was said in more allegorical terms by the mysterious *Stanzas of Dzyan*. Doubtless it could be stated in other ways as well. As Helena Blavatsky once put it, "These classifications are not hard and fast divisions. A term may change places according as the classification is exoteric, Esoteric, or practical. For students the effort should be to bring all things down to states of consciousness" (*The Secret Doctrine*, V:540/*The Esoteric Writings of H.P. Blavatsky*, Wheaton, IL: Theosophical Publishing House, 1980, pp. 445-46).

That is a key concept, for the crucial point is that for theosophy those *logoi* and their universes are first of all states of consciousness in interaction with matter. Mind, the child of that interaction, becomes many and clothes itself in robes of progressively denser matter. The bearers of these garments are the Pilgrims as they stream out of the womb of Mother Space on their great adventure of self-loss and self-discovery. Their several changes of garb will be our next topic.

THE SEVEN WORLDS

After the Pilgrims in their primordial joy—"when the sons of God shouted for joy," says the book of Job— have formed, they begin their pilgrimage. This requires vehicles; each of these corresponds to a world. (We now restrict our examples to the case of our own solar system and particularly our own Earth.)

The worlds through which the Pilgrims move are, in theosophical lore, seven in number. Three are worlds of descent or involution, made of successively denser—though to us still intangible—matter. Then comes our world of "solid" substance with its clearly focused distinctions in spirit-matter as we perceive it. Next come three worlds, on the same three "planes" as the descent, but now more refined, as the monad makes its evolution back again to the primordial Oneness, wisdom, and bliss, bearing with it treasures of experience to make the reunion all the richer.

This is the saga of the seven spheres which has preoccupied much traditional theosophical literature. It has filled many if not most readers with a

Principles and Corresponding Planes

		ENGLISH NAME	SANSKRIT NAME	CHARACTERISTICS
The Divine Trinity; The Three Logoi of Creation and "Divine Spark" Within Human Beings	1.	Essence, Being	Atma, Sat, Adi	Impersonal divine essence and extension; Will; Matter in the ultimate sense of primordial spirit / matter
	2.	Consciousness, Wisdom	Buddhi (as knowing or spirit), Chit, Prajna	Energizing; Matter-Spirit interplay; conscious awareness
	3.	Mind, expressed in activity and bliss	Manas (as universal mind), Ananda	The wave of individualized consciousness; the monad or Pilgrim nature; activity
The Globes of Involution / Evolution and Outer "Sheaths" of Human Beings	4.	Intuitive Globe and Sheath[1]	Buddhi	Ecstatic insight and realization; the highest reach of thought
	5.	Mental Globe and Sheath	Manas	Realm of rationality and thought[2]
	6.	Astral or Feeling Globe and Sheath	Kama	Realm of feelings[2]
	7.	Etheric / Physical Globe and Sheath	Prana Rupa	Physical realm and its energy-field

---

1. Just as the body is the seat or vehicle of all the higher human faculties, so the Earth (or other visible planet) is the physical embodiment of subtler levels of matter and energy which are universal in scope.
2. It must be remembered always that in the theosophical cosmology "thought" and "feeling" are at once a subjective state of consciousness and an appropriate state of energy or form.

confusing sense of complexity and abstraction, all the more so in that its specifics differ not a little from one source to another.

In pondering how to handle this material in the present book, I found myself torn between awareness of its strange and difficult quality on one hand, and a sense that some very important insight, however roughly expressed, lies behind it on the other. Because of the latter cognizance, I could not simply leave it alone. I finally decided to put forward a view of the globes and "life-waves" which is relatively simple and also modern in that it seeks to keep contemporary views of the universe and solar system in mind. It is not exactly the same as that of any earlier theosophical source. It is, however, quite compatible with that tradition, in my view, and I would like to think clarifies what the latter is trying to say. Keeping in mind Blavatsky's assertion that "these classifications are not hard and fast divisions" but capable of changing places, and her advice elsewhere that the teaching contains allegory and even "blinds," being of the nature of concepts to be worked through in a jnana yoga manner, I will presume to offer a model I hope some students will find helpful.

The teaching about the globes is significant if we think of it as an expression of fundamental principles of theosophy—the omnipresence of consciousness interacting with matter, evolution, periodicity. It tells us not only that these principles are true— with which many would agree in theory—but *how* they are true, how they have worked, in our particular case. The real excess of abstraction would be just to reiterate principles like evolution or periodicity without trying to apply them to what, for us, is the most crucial "real life" case, our world and our own adventure as conscious centers in it.

In considering this model of the globes and the planes of increasingly subtle states of matter in interplay with spirit, once more let us remind ourselves that these interpenetrate one another, as do the sheaths for living things created from them. The spirit/matter of the planes supplies the "stuff" of the various worlds through which we pass in involution and evolution, as well as the material for the various bodies or sheaths of each human being, who adds, as it were, a robe or sheath from each realm which he inhabits. Theosophical teaching says that as the life-wave sweeps through its involutionary sequence, the globe or world which is the major focus of life at that time becomes embodied in successively denser states of matter (or "supermatter," as it is not yet susceptible to physical senses). At the same time the globe retains embodiment in all the more subtle realms through which it has already gone. All these states of matter in which it is embodied interpenetrate and occupy the same space, much as water occupies the same space as a saturated sponge. Finally, the globe reaches the physical plane, after which it ascends plane by plane to higher states, dropping a level of embodiment at each stage as it climbs. This process goes through seven "rounds," and in each round one of the principles is emphasized in a manner appropriate for its expression at that stage.

The first three principles concern the Trinity with which we are familiar and do not constitute worlds and bodies as such. But they form the necessary triune "heart" of each world and sheath, around which as one or more of the four "lower" layers are added a body visible or invisible is made. The worlds

Involution and Evolution

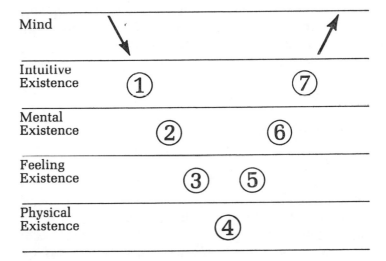

Being

Wisdom

Mind

Intuitive
Existence   ①   ⑦

Mental
Existence   ②   ⑥

Feeling
Existence   ③   ⑤

Physical
Existence   ④

Compare the chart in *The Secret Doctrine*, I:208/I:153. The entire process is well summarized a few pages later, in I:213-14/I:158-59. Note that sometimes, as here, somewhat the same process is looked upon from a much larger perspective as "rounds" in the life of a single globe which is part of a "chain" of interrelated worlds. But this is a technical matter which does not affect the basic principle of involution and evolution. It is said of the evolution of our Earth that "during the first three [rounds], it forms and consolidates; during the fourth, it settles and hardens; during the last three, it gradually returns to its first ethereal form; it is spiritualized, so to say."

or globes in which involution and evolution occur, then, form an arc.

Each world, as each principle, is in part a form of expression of the one next above it. The pivotal plane in a real sense is the third, Mind, Manas, articulated in activity and bliss. This is not yet the human mind but a universal principle that links the divine with the manifest. Mind and deep joy are overflowing aspects of God and at the same time the fundamental constituents of separate existence, both recalling manifestation to its divine nature and impelling it to express itself through activity in the various worlds. At this level of Mind, then, reality separates into monads or focal points of the One.

The Worlds of Involution

Here begins the pilgrimage of seemingly separate individuals. But the path individuals follow, it must be remembered, is exactly parallel to the way globes or worlds evolve on the larger scale. Man is the microcosm of the macrocosm. It may be difficult for us to conceive of something corresponding to intuition, thought, and feeling on a cosmic scale. Yet proponents of the Ancient Wisdom through the ages tell us that they are as real at the foundations of the universe as they are in human beings, for theosophy teaches that the cosmos is conscious, sensitive, and intelligent. What is said below from the perspective of human evolution also applies to evolution on the cosmic level.

The first state in which the monad or Pilgrim finds itself is that of intuition or creative insight. This "flashes off" divine joy and Mind deep within to present new ideas to consciousness; and the joy of creativity, with the joy of love which reflects the divine Unity here below, are the greatest joys separate existence can know.

In separate existence intuition must be "about" something. It must express itself in ideas, and ideas must not only be realized but also require remembering and analyzing. So comes the mental realm, which encompasses the human, rational faculties, depending on the intuitive yet also affording it scope for fuller expression.

In turn, ideas in interaction with other existences give rise to desires and fears as they crave fuller and fuller expression. To articulate this kind of expression, the feelings—for wonder, for beauty, for love, and yes also fear and anger on the lower levels—are gathered as robes about the Pilgrim.

Finally, it seems that feelings and the thoughts and intuitions behind them require a world of solid matter fully to express themselves—a world where beauty can be seen and painted, love consummated, fortresses built around fears, and stones thrown in anger. So it is that the Pilgrims of eternity make themselves worlds like the biblical "coats of skin" Adam and Eve sewed for themselves after their expulsion from the garden. Let us now look at these worlds of involution in more detail.

Globe One. The first is a world of the "stuff" of joyous insight, but with as yet very little to be insightful about, at least that we could comprehend, though the karmic ghosts of some high themes may carry over from previous universes. Each universe is after all one of an endless series, and the cycles by which they appear and disappear are like spirals rather than circles. Yet doubtless to us the first world would seem incredibly "thin," and indeed it is only a start for the pilgrimage, happy yet inchoate, the babbling happiness of babes first discovering themselves.

Globe Two. Eventually, following great laws of periodicity, the Pilgrims find themselves in another world, this one of mind or thought. The world and plane of mind is generally divided into two levels, the "higher" *manas* of "unformed" thought, described as a "flowing" or "sweeping" kind of mental activity, and the "lower" or "formed" *manas*, in which discrete objects of thought appear. Again, the nature of these thoughts, and the kind of images they evoke, is hard for us to imagine. Yet, like the intuitive impressions, they may have some content brought over from a previous universe, and they will not be wholly alien to us, for they are among the seeds of our world, having the same relation to our earth as seeds to flowers. They are that around which later the feelings and material structures of the planet will form.

Globe Three. Next comes the astral or feeling world on the corresponding plane. Use of the word "feeling" for this level, like many English terms for esoteric concepts, is very rough and in many ways misleading. If properly understood, the word "astral" may be better, though it has misled some into thinking it has a relation to physical stars, whereas the term refers to the "starry" or luminous character of the subtle substance associated with this plane.

The nature of the astral realm is hinted at by our experience of dreams and also by our experience with artistic creativity, for its keynote is the subjective impression of fluid harmony between inner feeling and the beautiful or disturbing world around us. It reverberates with organ-chords of feeling, from the most exalted apperceptions of aesthetic beauty or love to the nightmarish; it is too subtle to be thought of as emotion in the ordinary sense though a seedbed of what feeling means in our world.

The astral world, then, exhibits the Pilgrim-monad, the divine spark of the Trinity, now sheathed in intuitive, mental, and feeling robes of energy. The Pilgrim has now found a level offering everything but "solid" matter and its immediate accoutrements.

GLOBE FOUR: SOLID GROUND

Now comes the last great outward-bound state and the beginning of the return—the physical world. The intuitive, mental, and feeling robes now receive their logical topcoat—a material world through which what one intuits, thinks, and feels can be expressed in matter—physical love, painting with actual paint, hearing sound-wave music, fighting wars with solid swords and rockets and not just black magic.

We speak of this world as "solid," but of course it contains all the states of physical matter with which we are familiar—solids, liquids, gasses, as well as what theosophists call the "etheric" state. The last represents the energy field which is associated with biological organisms, and thus is characteristic of life. It surrounds our living planet but is especially localized around every living creature, signalling its state of energy and well-being. This field impinges on the yet subtler energies of the astral level, which psychics perceive as "auras," colors around a person in hues which reflect his spiritual and emotional states and which may contain both etheric and astral elements.

Also associated with the etheric, though said to form linkages between it and the astral plane, are the forces known in Sanskrit, Chinese, and Japanese as *prana*, *ch'i*, and *ki* respectively. *Prana* is spoken of extensively in connection with yoga, and *ch'i* and *ki* with the celebrated "martial arts" of China and

Japan. All these refer to an energy associated with life but spread throughout the universe, which can be directed and shaped by concentrated thought to effect results in the material plane. Prana is affected by emotion insofar as a strong emotion—whether of love or anger or fear—concentrates pranic power around a person experiencing it. (We say, for example, "I could feel that person's anger," or in the 1960s jargon talk about the "good vibes" put out by someone's love or peace.) But *prana* or *ch'i* is best governed by states of high yogic or meditative control of the mind and feelings rather than by any reactive emotional state, though it is the vehicle of emotion when it is generated.

I might add, for the millions who have seen the *Star Wars* series of movies, that the "Force" in them is very little different from *prana* or *ch'i*, the energy associated with the etheric in theosophy. In fact, the concept seems to have been inspired by the lore of the martial arts tradition in East Asia, where tales are numerous of samurai and other good and bad practitioners of the arts who could knock down a foeman by the energy of *ch'i* or *ki* alone, without physical contact, or use it to light a fire or move a heavy object at a great distance. In the same way, in India the *siddhis* or mysterious powers of a similar sort which yogis can develop are legendary; some use them only for good or set them aside as impediments to the highest spiritual realization, while others become fascinated by them and end up no more than black magicians.

It is significant to realize, in fact, that at each world-level the potential for evil as well as good exists. As the Pilgrims leave the unity of the One for their immense journey, the perspective of the One is veiled for them by the several planes of material existence already chronicled; the temptation is always to become attached to the pleasures and powers of the plane on which one is mainly focused. While it may not be entirely clear to us how one could sin on the intuitive, mental, or astral levels, it is not too hard to imagine selfish and exploitative "power games" on those levels, even the enslavement of an entire mental or astral sphere by a "black magician" of the mind or, in *Star Wars* talk, the "Dark Side of the Force." For we need not think that evil started in our world alone, or that its seeds, like those of life and thought, did not first germinate elsewhere. All this is part of what the Pilgrim, in the great quest, must contend with.

FROM OTHER WORLDS TO OUR EARTH

According to theosophy, what we experience as intuition, mind, and feeling is associated with some degree, however tenuous, of matter interacting with spirit. The monad itself is conceived of as spirit encased in a thin "film" of matter which takes on increasingly "thick" sheaths as it spirals downward through involution. Of course, the matter of these levels of consciousness and energy is not of the sort susceptible to the instruments of contemporary science; such susceptibility is the unique province of the matter of the fourth world, the physical, where science itself arose in response to its challenge. To discover the other planes and worlds, we must look within, using the mind as a test case to reveal its roots, rather than looking outward and using it as a searchlight.

Within each of the seven worlds or globes, the Pilgrims go through an evolution from the lowest forms possible on that plane to the highest, ending on that closest to the next one above and thus ready to make the leap to it. We know little about evolution on the first three worlds, save that it goes through "rounds" which, as we have seen, "touch base" with something of the nature of all seven planes that is appropriate to that globe.

On our world, however, the course of evolution is clearer, both from a theosophical and a palaeontological perspective. Theosophy postulates that life (that is, in scientific terms, energy) started on earth on the mineral level, as an "interiority" teeming with latent energy in what on the surface appears as inert matter, including the primordial "soup" of the first oceans. It moved up through the plant and animal kingdoms, becoming more and more characterized by the independence and intelligence of the individual over against the "group soul"* of the species. Finally the material it had evolved seemed ready for something more, the spark of true intelligence.

Here it is that the theosophical sources, especially The Secret Doctrine, make an unexpected move. Instead of saying, as one might have anticipated, that the Pilgrims of the earth who have moved up through the mineral, plant, and animal realms of this planet now break through into the human level of expression, it suddenly declares that they cannot make this great leap on their own. Indicating that their evolution thus far has been simply "nature's work" or evolutionary drive, the text says "Nature unaided fails," and tells us that our world at this point had outside help and even outside colonists.

---

*This is a term used in some later theosophical literature to indicate the evolutionary state of the monads which are as yet not completely individualized as human beings, as in minerals, plants, and animals.

Perhaps contemporary questions about the development of the human species can put this extraordinary assertion in perspective. How does one explain in evolutionary terms the remarkable leap from Pleistocene mammal to *homo sapiens,* with the latter's manifestation of a new kind of intelligence? How also explain that sense deep within us, that we are of the earth yet not wholly of it, children both of this oft-dark world and of starry heaven?

Theosophy tells us we indeed have enormously deep roots, both here and elsewhere—and that this is no unnatural thing, for in the whole solar system there is some cross-transferring of pilgrim ships, so that one does not finish the course on the same chain of worlds as one started. One may go through the intuitive, mental, and astral world-evolutions in one system, then switch to another "solid matter" world after it had been prepared by *its* pilgrim band from elsewhere. Presumably such transfers are as salutary as moving to a new city once or twice in one's career can be—we need new vistas to keep us fresh in spirit and to learn that we have "no abiding city" so long as we are on pilgrimage. Here, as elsewhere in theosophical lore, the individual must decide for himself the extent to which this account is literal or allegorical or even a "blind." However, fantastic as some may see it to be, it fits very well with the theosophical worldview being presented here, as well as explaining some mysteries not yet solved by science.

So it is, we are told, that the first "people" on Earth, from which we are descended at least psychically, were the Lunar Pitris or Moon Ancestors.

> The first root-race, *i.e.,* the first 'men' on earth (irrespective of form) were the progeny of the 'celestial men,' called rightly in Indian philosophy the 'Lunar Ancestors' or the Pitris, of which there

are seven classes or Hierarchies (*The Secret Doctrine* I:214/I:160).

In other words, the first men were Pilgrims who had undergone much of their pilgrimage on another, earlier chain of seven worlds, namely the Lunar. This was not on the moon as we know it, but a chain moving through the planes in a far-forgotten past, of which the dead sphere which turns its cracked face toward our planet is but a relic whose vitality has long left it and gone elsewhere.

> When a planet dies, its informing principles are transferred to a *laya* or sleeping center, with potential but latent energy in it, which is thus awakened into life and begins to form itself into a new sidereal body (*The Secret Doctrine* I:202/I:147).

These Lunar Ancestors came, according to *The Secret Doctrine*, before any mammal. This assertion, made very emphatically (III:176ff/II:168), flies in the face of evolutionary biology as science knows it, a fact which Blavatsky herself recognized. According to evolutionary theory, man is the *last* great step in mammalian evolution, apart from those forms such as domestic animals directly affected by human emergence. In terms of the fossil record, if man were the first mammal, he would have had to appear far back in the age of the dinosaurs, the Mesozoic.

A sensible theosophical solution exists for this apparent paradox. Suppose the Lunar Ancestors arrived amid the misty swamps of the reptilian era, or even at the dawn of life on Earth itself, not in a fully developed physical body but a body tenuously composed of astral or etheric elements, fluidic and insubstantial. For *The Secret Doctrine* projects "the birth of the astral before the *physical body:* the

former being a model for the latter" (III:15/II:1).
Furthermore:

> For, although the exact figures are withheld...
> one thing is clear, that the figures 18,000,000 of
> years, which embrace the duration of *sexual,
> physical* man, have to be enormously increased if
> the whole process of spiritual, astral and physical
> development is taken into account...Such ter-
> restrial conditions as were then operative [before
> the appearance of physical man] had no touch
> with the plane on which the evolution of the
> *ethereal astral* Races proceeded. Only in relatively
> recent geological periods, has the spiral course of
> cyclic law swept mankind into the lowest grade of
> physical evolution—the plane of gross material
> causation. In those early ages, *astral* evolution
> was alone in progress, and the two planes, the
> astral and the physical, though developing on
> parallel lines, had no direct point of contact with
> one another (III:164-65/II:156-57).

By "astral" here is meant the *Linga-sarira*, the subtle mold or model of the physical. In this ghostly
form the Lunar Pitris may have haunted our planet
for hundreds of millions of years, living lives dictated to them by the Cycle of Necessity (for had they
not been in need of much more development, they
would not have come to Earth). In their imperfect
way they may have indirectly stimulated the preparation of physical vessels appropriate to high intelligence. Indeed, the whole "life-wave" of Earth
came from the lunar chain, though in varying ranks,
the leading edge being presumably the human proto-
type, the Lunar Pitris.

The implication is that when the lunar world
"died," these Pilgrims were not yet ready to leave the
fourth, "solid-matter" world experience. They came
here to find bodies, but first dwelt only in astral or

(more likely) etheric form, since suitable bodies had not yet appeared, nor suitable physical brains. In the plant and animal kingdoms *manas* is largely dormant. *The Secret Doctrine* says of the Moon Ancestors' Earth, "Man remained an empty senseless Bhuta"—the Hindu term for ghost. These life-forms were hermaphrodite, as apparently are Pilgrims in the intuitive, mental, and astral worlds, sexual division and reproduction being a characteristic only of fully embodied fourth-world creatures.

The Coming of the Solar Pitris

Development on Earth under the Sons of the Moon and their cousin Pilgrims struggling up through the material kingdoms was painfully slow. Whether this planet would ever make the breakthrough on its own to higher intelligence was much in doubt for "Nature unaided fails." At this low point, it appears, passage through the Cycle of Necessity requires an outside "push" to spark the sluggish *manas* now slumbering within matter at its densest, and establish momentum for the upward return.

Fortunately, that help is available. A solar system is centered in a Solar Logos, a sublime embodiment of the divine Trinity in manifest form, answering for all intents and purposes to the wise, benign God of religion within its sphere, exalted above the worlds and the struggling creatures wheeling around it. Moreover, this felicitous deity has associated with it legions of high angelic beings, lords who have successfully completed the Cycle in an earlier world-chain of this system, but chosen to remain with it out of compassion for those still laboring upward. They have many titles, among them Lords of the Flame,

Sons of Wisdom, Kumaras (Holy Youths), Manas-aputras (Sons of Mind).

According to theosophical lore, some 18 million years ago a company of these higher beings accelerated Earth's evolution. Some awakened the *manas* or mind principle; others incarnated in a portion of the human race to encourage its growth.

We may infer that at this point the Lunar Pitris, under the stimulation of the great awakening brought by these beings, took wholly physical bodies prepared for them by animal evolution. *The Secret Doctrine* indicates that "the fivefold Lha," a Tibetan term referring to the Solar Pitris, "completed" man, and that "Nature concreted the present physical body" around the etheric framework of the Lunar Pitris.

The figure of 18 million years need not be taken too literally, though we shall see in the next chapter that it may approximately mark an important juncture in the evolution of proto-human forms. Here, however, we want to stay with the "big picture" of worlds and planes. What happens next after the full incarnation of intelligence on pilgrimage in the fourth world of dense matter?

How long we remain on this globe hereafter is indeterminate. We can see our future only very faintly. Indeed it may depend in no small degree on choices we are now making or will make, for while the chain proceeds by pattern it should not be thought of deterministically. It may be *we* who decide whether for our pilgrim band life in the fourth world of dense matter is quickly transcended or lasts as long as this material universe, or even longer.

Eventually it will be transcended. As we have seen, some may move rapidly ahead of the group, to the benefit of all, but the great mass of Pilgrims will move more or less together, creating fresh worlds in the process. The fifth world, on the return, will be astral, the sixth mental, and the seventh intuitional. Thus they duplicate in their hierarchical nature the worlds through which life descended during involution into the dense matter of the fourth world.

Through involution consciousness becomes more individualized, less inchoate and diffuse, as matter becomes denser. Then, through evolution back up the trail, unity is slowly regained, but with the sharp individualized focus retained, allowing more clarity, conscious understanding, and awareness than on the way down. In involution the globes were learning experiences, ways in which we as Pilgrims prepared ourselves for incarnation in our present earth.

On the way back we will pass through emotional, mental, and intuitional worlds in order to develop their potential for expression far more fully, on the basis of what has been learned while outward bound. Ultimately, we will transcend the limitations of each one of these, thereby enabling our return to the Unconditioned Reality of the One. In the process we become as gods, like the Dhyani-Chohans or Lords of the Flame and other great beings, able to help those further down the path. Or we may move on to "inner" work or unimaginable duties in other worlds and universes, before the ultimate return.

THE MEANING OF THE SEVEN WORLDS FOR TODAY

This, then, is the theosophical scenario concerning cosmic evolution. Much in this picture, needless to say, remains obscure. It is really little more than a hint at something vast and significant in the far background of human life here and now. But those hints are treasures beyond price. They show us that, despite the trials and frustrations of the passing day, our lives are parts of something tremendously grand and joyous.

Even now we *are* evolving, evolving through and beyond the fourth world. It is a vast drama, and each act plays on for a long time; there is sufficient time, which is encouraging when we think of our many failures. On the other hand, the story is an ongoing one and we ourselves can help to set its pace. This stimulates us to do our best to be worthy of better states of life and higher levels of service.

Everything, however seemingly insignificant, is a part of the plot. Every friendly smile at a neighbor is a mini-enlightenment. It helps set the stage for the next subtle material world, the astral, by creating a kindly, benign form on that level. Every high thought of beauty and love looks far ahead, as through a wizard's telescope, up to the sixth world, the realm of pure insight. The play may be long, but it keeps moving and the plot is thickly packed. There's never a moment totally insignificant to its ultimate climax.

Note again that this drama is really a history of the evolution of awareness, to which the worlds are accessories. Some may think it fanciful, and to be sure little can be adduced as proof of it, save what one learns by looking inward, or hears from the lips of those accounted wise. Yet nothing about it is incredible either, if one accepts the basic theosophical premises that mind is not to be explained simply as a material product, and that our inner self is sufficiently different from the world's material surfaces that it must have a separate origin and history.

The narrative I have given is simply that history. It shows that, prior to union with our bodily forms, our mind and feeling components developed through various states and worlds, and this helps us understand some of our deepest perceptions about the nature of our conscious minds. If mind has a separate history at all, something must have happened in that history to make our minds what they are in fact, and not something else. It seems to me that the theosophical history of those happenings fits well with much of human experience.

One could, of course, argue that the soul of each newborn babe is a special, immediate creation. But that makes no more sense than to say that the physical body of the baby is a wholly new creation. To be sure, each baby, like each mind, is unique. But the baby would not be there without the genetic patterns brought over from the father and mother, traceable back through millions of years of the development of life on earth.

In the same way, the baby's mind—though superficially unformed at birth—will display deep capacities and patterns, for intuitional joy, for formless and formed thought, for linkage with feeling and other invisible energies, which point, in the theosophical view, to a very long career on subtler worlds. The baby will also soon show distinctive patterns of behavior and attitudes which cannot wholly be explained by his hereditary factors or by his environment in this life, and which theosophists would say are the result of karma carried over from other lifetimes.

The baby being born, like the aged man dying in another room of the same hospital, is taking a step in a great pilgrimage. With each step the Pilgrim is learning much, and before the journey is over will achieve a great task: learning how to know what he has learned.

3
The Human Experience

A Play Within the Play

Now we continue the saga of the cosmic Pilgrims who have become human beings, fully clothed with flesh of dense matter, on planet Earth. The human story on Earth is a drama on a much smaller scale than the sequence of worlds and the prehuman Earth we considered in the last chapter, a play within the play. But the small scale is only relative; we are still talking about millions of years of human experience, and the cycles of which we shall speak will dwarf —and put into perspective—the rise and fall of nations and empires which preoccupy "ordinary" history books.

We have explored two keynotes of this drama—the original arrival of a life-wave including humans, or perhaps one should say potential humans, from the lunar worlds far back when the earth was much younger than today, and the coming of higher beings to catalyze the evolution of human minds and forms as we know them now.

The fundamental category for the further understanding of human development, from the theosophical perspective, is the concept of "Root Races." Like the worlds, these are seven in number.

We should say at the outset that they have at the most only a very marginal relation to the physiological types of present-day humanity. Although they represent great cumulative stages of human development, they also do not parallel the anthropological levels of cultural attainment, which are largely based on the type of artifacts made and the methods of food-gathering, such as the Paleolithic and Neolithic.

Rather, like all theosophical ideas at root, they derive ultimately from the fundamental conviction that consciousness is basic to manifestation through its interplay with matter. The races represent subtle, inward stages in the development of consciousness in its adaptation to physical existence on this planet. That process is reflected in outward appearances—but it must be remembered that mirrors often distort and mislead.

Each so-called Root Race indicates a major phase of development in human consciousness in interaction with our material world. Each persists for a long period of time, going through cycles of development and decline, during which it manifests seven distinct subtypes or subdivisions. But we are now little more than halfway through the process, and the true meaning of what has gone on, and is now going on in human history, will undoubtedly be but poorly ascertained until the end, when all strands are gathered up. Then beings far wiser than we—or rather ourselves far wiser than now—will look back on thousands of centuries as on a tapestry whose weaving is done, and comment on the strange and intricate intertexturing and the complex beauty of the whole.

Let us now outline this theosophical model of

human development. The First Root Race appeared on earth at a time when the planet was still in a formative state and life was just emerging in the primal "soup." This would be the Pilgrims from the lunar chain of worlds, Pilgrims who as yet still had no full physical existence. Theirs has been called an etheric race because the bodies of its folk were composed of that subtler, more fluid and less dense organic substance. This Race represents the first adaptations of Pilgrims seeking the experience of earthly existence.

The Second Root Race was called by H.P. Blavatsky in *The Secret Doctrine* the Hyperborean. These people had loose-knit watery bodies, presumably also etheric, and inhabited a continent on the northern part of our globe, at a time when the land-masses were quite different from those of our era. What is now known about continental drift and polar shift supports to some degree theosophical belief that the configuration of land on earth has changed greatly throughout its long past. The Hyperboreans' land is said to have been balmy in climate, but the inhabitants took remarkably diverse and monstrous shapes with their fluid etheric bodies, as they experimented with the mysterious world of physical existence.

The first two Root Races reproduced by dividing, and thus enjoyed an amoeba-like immortality. Little is known of their consciousness, but certainly it was primitive, the manas being largely latent.

It is in the Third Root Race, the Lemurian, that humanity began to take form as we now know it. In it division into male and female, and sexual reproduction, commenced. It was in the middle of the Lemurian period that the higher beings arrived to aid nature, to enable our wraith-like precursors to take fully physical form, and to spark the evolution of human intelligence.

According to theosophical lore, the Lemurians in-

habited a continent in what are now the South
Pacific and Indian oceans. They are presumably
ancestral to the peoples who later occupied Africa
and parts of Asia, areas where the earliest human
and humanoid remains have been found.

It is unwise to press too much convergence of
theosophical and current scientific perspectives. The
latter is prone to change, and we do not know the full
purport of the former. Nonetheless, it is interesting
to note that the first identifiable antecedent of man
according to some authorities is Ramapithecus,
known from fossil remains in the foothills of the
Himalayas dating back some 14 to 16 million years.
This is close to that point in the middle of the Lemurian era when, according to theosophical sources,
humanity with outside help took full physical form
and began a direct evolutionary march to where we
are now.

It is also interesting that continental drift theory
now holds that one of the most recent plates to move
into its present location is that of the Indian subcon-
tinent. It was separated from the Asian mainland
and far out in the Indian Ocean, the traditional location of Lemuria, as late as 20 or 30 million years ago;
around the former date it rammed into Asia, pushing
skyward the world's highest mountains, the Himalayas, in whose lower ranges the remains of Ramapithecus long awaited modern discovery.

Regarding Lemurian consciousness, the accounts
are characteristically more spotty. We are told in *The
Secret Doctrine* that conditions varied. Most Lemurians were quite primitive, though apparently ruled by
kings and able to build massive but crude cities. At
the same time, they possessed psychic powers
which, far from exceptional or repressed as today,
were considered normal and put to everyday use.

Their religion was a simple uninstitutionalized monotheism. But among them, a small "elect," led by higher beings, incarnated in human form to guide the development of the race, kept deep wisdom alive in secret lodges. To what extent all this may be accepted as literal truth and to what extent as merely symbolic of the exceptional creativity and social organization, and the remarkable potential, of creatures normative anthropology would regard as still only prehuman, the reader must deliberate. (*The Secret Doctrine* III:316-19/II:316-19) As the Lemurians declined, their "elect" including those embodied higher beings are said to have retreated to Shambhala, a mysterious site in the Gobi desert.

The Fourth Root Race is the Atlantean, a name derived from the celebrated lost continent of Atlantis of which Plato spoke. However, *The Secret Doctrine* says the name refers "not to Plato's island alone" but to several areas of the earth (III:322/II:322), and in fact the arising of the Atlanteans seems to be more or less coeval with the appearance of the first hominids in Eastern and Southern Africa whose fossil remains dating back some 4 million years have recently been found.

The Atlanteans, arising from Lemurian remnants, were divided between a warrior race and a "pious, meditative race" (*The Secret Doctrine* III:370/II:371). At the outset both were, each in its own way, "deeply versed in primeval wisdom and the secrets of nature," though antagonistic. They pursued a "double evolution." There are somewhat cryptic hints that no small technological advance occurred in this era: the use of fire, the building of cities, the development of metallurgy, and on the part of the "pious" race with its peaceful ways recurrent visits by "gods."

But the Atlanteans, like the Lemurians before them, eventually declined, fell into evil ways, and at last saw most of their civilization destroyed by a great cataclysm, the deluge of which ancient literature speaks. Remnants of the island empire, however, established the roots of later culture on both sides of the Atlantic.

Again the narrative can doubtless be interpreted on several levels of exoteric fact and esoteric myth; let the reader decide what seems best. Taken with a grain of common sense, however, there is nothing too improbable about the Atlantean scenario as a parable of the first few million years of protohumanity and humanity. Those were times when the first truly human technologies and societies were slowly evolving, and experience with tribal peoples today illustrates that some can be vehemently warlike and others almost unbelievably gentle and peaceful folk who devote much attention to ceremonial and mystical matters; compare the "Dionysian" and "Apollonian" societies described in Ruth Benedict's classic *Patterns of Culture*.

As for religious values, in a sense Atlanteans, both pacific and otherwise, were more "psychic" than we. They were closer to the etheric mode of existence humanity had known up to the middle of the Lemurian era. Like their predecessors, though increasingly less so, they retained vestiges of a protophysical state in which astral and etheric (i.e., "psychic") modes of communication and activity were commonplace. It is as though they were more at home with such ancient vehicles than with their still-novel fleshly forms.

Yet as the Atlantean age progressed, that capacity took a dark form, probably because its heyday was passing. Tensions between it and the demands of a new, more fully material mode of experience were rising—a mode with its own capacity for good and ill. But to hold to that whose time has past in a particular form of expression inevitably leads to evil, as when an adult refuses to give up childish ways or a modern nation refuses progress toward human rights. So it was that the last of the Atlanteans fell into low magic and sorcery, the perversion for the ends of power and exploitation of psychic and spiritual realities.

This may have been especially the temptation of the "pious," for the profoundest temptations are really spiritual rather than physical, and the devout are especially susceptible to them. But when the destroying and purifying waves finally rolled over Atlantis, we are told, it was the baleful sorcerers of the "Dark Face" who largely perished beneath them and a remnant of the righteous who escaped, even as millions of years before a remnant had fled when Lemuria was largely devastated by subterranean fires.

THE FIFTH ROOT RACE

Those who departed Atlantis (whatever that fabled name exactly represents) became the nucleus of the Fifth Root Race, the Aryan. Their epoch, now in midcourse, began perhaps a million years ago and so covers the span, in exoteric anthropology, of material human culture from the first flint blades to the spaceship. In terms of consciousness, it indicates a stage during which humankind becomes fully at home in the material realm, learns how it works, how to use it as a vehicle for expression, how through it to know and love Ultimate Reality as the ideal of knowledge and beauty. Its great temptation is to regard one's human self as also no more than material.

The Aryan and other Root Races must be seen as

levels in the development of human consciousness in interaction with our material world, the Fifth Race being the most deeply engaged with "dense" matter. As stages of consciousness, the Races affect all human consciousness one way or another. Theosophical literature brings out strongly that much overlap may be found between successive Root Races and that in practice they are thoroughly intermingled, so that no human group today represents a "pure" race—a point also made by anthropologists.

In particular, we must stress that the theosophical use of the term "Aryan" for the Fifth Root Race is quite different from its much later use by German National Socialism with all the ugly connotations lent that term by Nazi evil. The word is originally Sanskrit and simply means "noble"—in the Buddhist scriptures it is applied to all those of spiritual sincerity, regardless of race. More fundamentally, in theosophy Aryan, like other Root Race names, simply applies to a particular kind of emerging human consciousness: if it happens to be especially articulated by one actual people or another at one time, that is no more than a transitory historical function within the Plan. It has nothing to do with intrinsic racial superiority or inferiority. In a striking passage, H.P. Blavatsky said in *The Secret Doctrine:*

> If tomorrow the continent of Europe were to disappear and other lands to re-emerge instead, and if the African tribes were to separate and scatter on the face of the earth, it is they who, about a hundred thousand years hence, would form the bulk of the civilized nations. And it is the descendants of those of our highly cultured nations, who might have survived on some one island, without any means of crossing the new seas, that would fall back into a state of relative savagery. Thus the

reason given for dividing humanity into *superior* and *inferior* races falls to the ground and becomes a fallacy. (III:423/II:425)

Another theosophical classic, *The Mahatma Letters to A.P. Sinnett*, vividly expresses the transitoriness of each people's day in the sun:

> When your Race—the fifth—will have reached its zenith of *physical* intellectuality, and developed the highest civilization (remember the difference we make between *material* and *spiritual* civilizations), unable to go any higher in its own cycle, its progress toward *absolute* evil will be arrested (as its predecessors the Lemurians and Atlanteans, the men of the third and fourth Races were arrested in their progress toward the same) by one of such cataclysmic changes; its great civilization destroyed, and all the subraces of *that* Race will be found going down their respective cycles, after a short period of glory and learning. See the remnants of the Atlanteans—the old Greeks and Romans (the modern all belong to the fifth Race); see how great and how short, how evanescent were their days of fame and glory! For, they were but subraces of the seven off-shoots of the "Root Race." No mother Race, any more than her subraces and off-shoots, is allowed by the one Reigning Law to trespass upon the prerogatives of the Race or sub-race that will follow it; least of all—to encroach upon the knowledge and powers in store for its successor. (pp.153-54)

(Here we note, incidentally, how overlapping the situation of actual peoples is; although the Aryan race or stage may have begun a million years before, the ancient Greeks and Romans are still spoken of as remnants of the Atlanteans. *The Secret Doctrine*, probably better, speaks of them as a complex mixture of Fourth and Fifth Root Race strains. [IV:312-13/ II:311-13])

Aryan religious consciousness has had to come to terms with the Fifth Race's calling to explore and exploit the material realm. That task has required the development—disproportionate development, from an ultimate point of view—of the objective, scientific kind of knowledge. In religion, objectification has led to the projection of the divine as other than world and self, eventuating in transcendant monotheism and legalistic styles of religious behavior. Yet our original psychic and mystical faculties are still there, latent. But apart from the case of a few exceptional people, they are able to break through only in occasional bursts, often of an inchoate, confusing sort.

Psychic and mystical gifts, if used in a spirit of humility and love, are an excellent thing. Yet they will not be the major focus of our civilization— indeed are likely to remain a provocative but puzzling sideline for most people—because as part of the Great Plan we are now intended mainly to experience something else, the fullness of embodiment and all its wonders. Those gifts are at once a throwback to a distant past and a harbinger of the future. They remind us of when we and our way of being in the world had not yet "solidified" so much as now, and they foretell, after our present initiation in the realm of matter is done, of distant births as masters of many dimensions and horizons.

THE MEANING OF ROOT RACES

What are we to make of this teaching about the evolution of human consciousness put in terms, at least partly metaphorical, of successive though overlapping races? The overall picture is not hard to grasp: a primal impetus from the higher beings; a slow adjustment to embodiment while psychic gifts flourished, as freely used as telephones and television by us; a new age deeply split between mystic warriors and mystic pacifists, which finally ended in sorcery as a debased people clung too long to the psychic tools of a dying epoch; then the slow rising of a brand of humans somewhat more at home in the strictly material world, more given to objective knowledge and to the technologies of nuts and bolts than to dreams and wizardries—though he may have borrowed some of his craft from the lost arts of sunken Atlantis.

Little can be proven about the states of consciousness of times past. Stones and bones survive, but of that evidence most indicative of human consciousness, most of the art and all the songs and stories of millions of years past are lost forever. As with the globes of theosophical lore, to know and understand what early human states of consciousness were really like, one has best to look within, to the far memory lodged within our deepest inward channels of awareness, to see what we recognize of this past human consciousness which so far antedates most of that which ordinary anthropology can speak. If, in looking in and back, we find those ancient sages, savages, and sorcerers, and those dawn-children of the Fifth Race first looking on the world with knowing eye, then the story may not be without meaning for us. Before proceeding, though, a few basic statements about the teaching on Root Races may be in order.

First, this doctrine is, perhaps more than any other major area of theosophical lore, given to us in fragmentary and veiled form. Gaps appear, much is left unsaid, and indications are that some of it is in the form of metaphor and poetic imagery. No single assertion about it should be taken as the whole or final truth; as with so much in theosophical teaching, its real value is in the vistas it opens and the inner connections it excites us into fusing for ourselves.

Second, let us emphasize again that this teaching can be used to establish no doctrine of racial superiority, but rather describes a chain of experiences through which all of us have passed. The cornerstone of the theosophical attitude is the ideal of human brotherhood, expressed in the first object of the Society, "To form a nucleus of the Universal Brotherhood of Humanity, without distinction of race, creed, sex, caste, or color." Any teaching contrary to this ideal, or which mitigates its spirit, is untheosophical, no matter where found. For in their divine essence all humans are equal, regardless of bodily form or cultural setting they happen to be experiencing at the moment, or to what sex or religion they are temporarily subject.

In fact, traditional theosophical doctrine holds that each individual self has been incarnated several times not only in each Root Race but in each of the forty-nine subdivisions, seven for each Race. In *The Mahatma Letters* the statement is made that each person must evolve through every Race and every one of its branches (p. 81). When we speak about the role of any race, then, we are really talking about ourselves, for we embody them all in our experience and our own consciousness. If we denigrate any, we denigrate ourselves. All Races, like all persons, have a common origin, and each has a unique role to play in human history and human life; all equally have lessons to learn. On the other hand, each has its lessons to teach, for, as we have seen, all have had their wise sages, and in each a high master has incarnated as spiritual guide.

COMING ROOT RACES

Where do we go from here? If this pattern is valid and we are now in the midst of the Fifth Root Race in the earthly cycle, we have two more great phases, the Sixth Root Race and the Seventh. We are told that the sixth subrace of the Fifth Root Race, out of which the Sixth Root Race will ultimately stem, is beginning to emerge now, some say centered in the "melting pot" of America.

As we have indicated, the era of each Root Race ends with a great cataclysm that seems to destroy civilization, or at least the best of it. Yet there are always survivors who construct a new culture in another part of the globe, and this will eventually rise to a higher level than the previous. The cataclysm is not brought about by natural forces alone, for it is linked to the moral decline of the Root Race as it reaches the end of its cycle.

Our Fifth Root Race is only a little past the midpoint of its cycle according to *The Secret Doctrine*. But even if our civilization were destroyed by atomic or other catastrophe of our own making, we can have faith that something of humanity would survive—no doubt chastened by such a terrible lesson—and that ultimately the civilization of the Sixth Root Race will arise to attain a splendor beyond our present imaginings. Nonetheless, it too will have its problems, some of them to be resolved by the Seventh Race in the still more distant future. For even if the gross evils of war, violence, poverty, and blatant inequity, which are still all too much with us, are finally resolved by the Sixth Root Race, issues of inner fulfillment and their relation to society, of which we have a glimmer, will doubtless arise.

Three final notes about the Root Races. First, we must never fall into the trap of viewing the theosophical cycles of history deterministically. Although they represent likely patterns, linked as they are to larger cosmic cycles and the collective karma of earth, they do not override individual freedom or moral choice. The choice is always ours. Nothing prevents our avoiding another decline and cataclysm if we so choose, or transmuting it into an inner initiation to a higher moral level rather than projecting it outwardly as natural or nuclear holocaust. Nothing prevents our accelerating past rates of evolution many, many times to make earth a paradise within one generation. (As a matter of fact, the world around us seems to be changing at a faster rate than ever before, and this speeding up is suggested by the teaching found in some theosophical sources that the time alloted each successive Root Race is shorter than the preceding. In this view the Lemurians had over 17 million years, the Atlanteans several million and the Aryans thus far have had only about one million and are already past midpoint.)

Second, let us remind ourselves again that we really know very little about the reasons for what has appeared thus far in human history. Whether on this or some other world, human history as we know it is only beginning. Our words about ultimate human destiny are like the talk of fond parents wondering what their toddler will be like as an adult. Doubtless higher guardians look upon our present struggles as we view the efforts of babes to walk and talk. From them we can and do glean a few hints regarding what our lives are all about—hints which, however, we may understand little better than a child understands the conversation of adults.

Third, in connection with the Root Races, and also the theory of globes discussed earlier, we have asked the reader to look within to see if confirmation can be found on some deep level of consciousness. Modern readers, attuned to the outlook of Freudian psychoanalysis, may wonder whether this introspection might not actually bring up only impressions carried over from early childhood, or even the womb. The way we have described those earlier modes of human existence could well fit with the veiled but potent "memories" we have of the first stages of life—the dark, warm, floating world of the womb, the magical, feeling-centered world of the infant and young child.

This critique is interesting and deserves consideration. But only the most rigorously reductionistic psychoanalysts are likely to think it closes the case. For that explanation does not tell *why* we follow this sort of individual developmental pattern in the first place, or indeed why we are here with human consciousness at all. True, early life on the intuitive, mental, and astral globes may embody experiences parallel to those of the nascent, seemingly disembodied foetus in the womb as it slowly gathers its mental and emotional capacities, and the earlier Root Races may match the experience of the infant and toddler as his primal panpsychic consciousness gradually fades and he grows accustomed to life in an earth-body and exchanges "magical" for "rational" understanding of how the world works. But what if it is a matter of "ontogeny follows phylogeny," the biological rule that the development of the embryo and infant follows the overall evolution of the species? In the human case, the foetus recapitulates human physical evolution, from fish to simian. Why then should not consciousness follow the way consciousness has evolved, if the theosophical model is correct, in the earlier globes and Root Races? More that "clicks" is interpreted by the theosophical picture than by the reductionistic.

WHAT ARE THESE HUMAN BEINGS?

What is the essential nature of human beings as they pass through the successive experiences of earthly life? The theosophical concept centers around three interrelated principles: the sheaths, karma, and reincarnation. In other words, we are a complex of seven interpenetrating kinds of "stuff," from the divine essence to the dense physical; we are affected by the universal law of cause and effect which operates on the moral and mental as well as the material levels; and, in accordance with the dictates of that law, we pass from one physical vehicle to another lifetime after lifetime.

Let us first review the theosophical teaching about the sheaths. The basic idea is that, since we are manifestly complex beings who simultaneously experience life physically, emotionally, mentally, and spiritually—with intricate gradations and combinations in between—we can think of ourselves as having several "bodies" all at once: the material, the emotional, the mental, and spiritual. These bodies or sheaths correspond to the principles, human and cosmic, outlined in the chart on page 68. They can be thought of as made up of different refinements of the cosmic substance, consciousness in interaction with matter, appropriate to the function they perform, though they flow into one another and influence one another. Such language is largely metaphorical, but for theosophists it provides the best "pointers" available for an in-depth look at what it means to be that wonderful and many-layered piece of work known as a human being.

Starting from "outside" (to use another metaphor), we have the "dense" physical body—solids, liquids, gases, and, according to theosophy, the "etheric double" or energy field interpenetrating it and closely approximating its form. In part, this probably corresponds with the electrical field, recently captured in Kirlian photography, that is part of a living organism. Theosophy would go beyond that, however, to say that it serves as a kind of mold for the physical body, linking the physical to the "higher" mental and spiritual bodies, and transmitting subtle energies between them. As the field of *ki* or *prana*, the etheric can also be manipulated by trained individuals to activate and exercise life energy within and outside the body.

Next is the astral or feeling sheath. It is the medium of feeling from the most subtle aesthetic level to the most sensual on its "lower" levels. Here sensory input is received and "digested" in accordance with the overall karmic condition and spiritual state of the individual, and here are shaped the astral forms which serve as the archetypes activating its desires.

The mental or manasic sheath is usually divided into two levels, the "lower" which is concerned with memory and the ordinary problem-solving and reactive kind of thought, and the "higher" which might be said to be engaged in "thought for its own sake"—metaphysical, free, exploratory thought.

Some theosophical writers have gone so far as to say that the lower and higher manas, though like two sides of the same coin, for that very reason face opposite directions, as though toward opposing poles. The lower manas faces the material world, and deals with our problems and responses in regard to it. The higher manas faces the spiritual world and endeavors to raise us to it. To put it another way, the lower manas, by the nature of its task, objectifies and deals with objective reality; the higher deals in subjectivity, the more ultimate reality, and at its best knows without objectifying its knowledge into frozen words and concepts.

At that point the manas substance begins to flow into the next, the buddhic or intuitional. This represents the "stuff" underlying the ecstatic flashes of realization associated with inward joy—both the deep motivation of all thought and the subtlest level of separate existence. Since it is beyond the normal range of the lower manas's objective thought, we do not know much *about* it; its nature is not easily put into our usual vocabulary, but it is there, like the light behind the eye.

That is all the more true of the three highest forms of expression, Being, Consciousness, and Mind or Bliss. They are the divine Trinity within reflecting the cosmic, our ultimate nature and our inward highway to the oneness of the universe. Yet we mostly know of these levels through their manifestations on more familiar planes, and then only if we are perceptive enough to have amid those manifestations, in the words of the poet,

> . . . a sense sublime
> Of something far more deeply interfused,
> Whose dwelling is the light of setting suns,
> And the round ocean and the living air,
> And the blue sky, and in the mind of man;
> A motion and a spirit, that impels
> All thinking things, all objects of all thought,
> And rolls through all things.
> Wordsworth, "Tintern Abbey"

Nonetheless, through the cultivation of introspection and meditation we can, I believe, find those moments in which we know whereof we speak when we speak of the highest things.

To continue with the theosophical conceptual framework concerning human nature, the pattern I have outlined breaks down into three parts (see the chart on page 68). The most obvious is the actual physical body. Next comes a personality field composed of the etheric, astral, and lower mental sheaths, closely connected with the dense physical form and concerned with its day-to-day interaction with its environment. Finally there is a "higher" part comprised of the Trinity itself plus the intuitional and "higher" mental levels. This indwells and, if the terms may be allowed, activates or inspires the ordinary mind, feeling, and physical operation of the lower selves, yet does not participate directly in them.

The "higher" part does not deliberate getting up each morning or how to handle the day's business, though in a deep sense its very presence, and our desire to touch and express this level, keeps us going; whatever we do of creativity or love is inspired however unconsciously by the divine within.

In the striking image of the Upanishads, these two parts are like "two birds of golden plumage," sitting side by side on a branch, one looking around and eating the fruits of the world, the sweet and bitter fruits, the other just quietly observing. We have within ourselves these two parts: the eater and doer, and the observer.

For theosophy this distinction is extremely important. The "observer" or "watcher"—the Trinity, buddhic, and higher manas levels—may be called the soul or, more technically, the causal body. It is the

Pilgrim which passes through reincarnation from one physical-feeling-lower mental vehicle to another. It is called "causal" because it is the "cause" of such a body's coming into being, and it gives that body its fundamental characteristics.

Because the causal body subsumes and gives rise to the physical form, feelings, memory, and ordinary mind, these features are not carried over from one life to another. We do not, therefore, usually remember things from previous lives, nor necessarily look the same, feel the same, or think the same on "practical" levels from one life to the next. What does carry over, embedded in the higher manas and even the intuitional level, is a certain *style* of thought, an underlying subjective character, that would link the two incarnations in the eyes of the wise.

KARMA

We pass from life to life like a ship slipping along with the current of a great river, the river of karma. We have already noted that karma means action with its cause-and-effect. From the theosophical point of view, and the Eastern generally, karma is an obvious truth, as clear in the moral and spiritual sphere as is gravity in the physical.

Just as a stone thrown into a pond will send out ripples which expand until the energy is expended or the bank is reached, so every thought, word, and deed produces karmic reactions. Those of selfishness perpetuate individual self-existence, living for self with all its limitations and pain, and those of love link us with the oneness of all things. On a more intermediate level, karma tells us that all we are and do prepares us for all we will be, in a process so vast

that it is beyond the power of any human mind to
grasp more than bits of it here and there. Yet we can
understand causes set into motion in one life that
need to be carried forward in another as the causal
body is wafted by karma from form to form—a gift
not fully developed, a contradiction not resolved,
two intertangled lives that need to work some problems through, a debt that needs to be paid.

All these kinds of things, down to the smallest
determinant of where and when and to whom the
new birth will come, karma prepares. It does not,
however, do more than set the stage—and often it
keeps setting it, year after year. How well we play the
part is up to us. Maybe we do it so well that we get a
thunderous ovation and go on to a much better role,
or maybe we have to rehearse the same lines over
and over.

In the big picture, then, karma is like a stream, an
energy process which carries the Pilgrim from role
to role in accordance with what each role has set in
motion. Karma is not so much "in" the causal body
as its conveyor. Much of the karma conveying each
causal body is individually generated, but it is well to
realize this is not all. There is also such a thing as
group karma: the karmas of families, communities,
nations, the world itself, created by their collective
behaviors. Group karma can impinge on the destiny
of all individuals within these groups, particularly
larger destinies such as war and peace, famine or
prosperity.

AFTER DEATH

The way sheaths and karmic forces work can be illustrated by a description of one of the most interest-

ing of theosophical teachings, that concerning what happens after one shuffles off the mortal coil. From the theosophical point of view, that is *all* that happens at death—the remaining components continue as before but more vividly, no longer constrained in their astral, mental, and higher life by the weight of dense matter, though also unable to experience reality directly through the medium of matter.

At first even the etheric body remains. We are told that what happens immediately at physical death is that the "etheric double" withdraws from the physical form, carrying with it the "higher" sheaths. Only a slender line of force, the "silver cord," links it to the body in life. In the last moments of life in that physical body, the events of life pass over the screen of consciousness, a matter known to folk wisdom especially in connection with drowning. Then "the silver cord is broken" at the moment of actual death.

Much recent research on "near death experiences," such as that popularized in Raymond Moody's *Life After Life*, has confirmed the overall picture presented by theosophy of the separation of the etheric double, insofar as one can rely on accounts of people who have virtually "died" but then returned to life in the body. In theosophical terminology, they would be people whose etheric form (together with the higher sheaths) has left the physical body as at death, but then re-entered. This can occasionally happen, apparently, in sleep, under anesthesia, and in what parapsychologists call "out of the body" experiences as well. Thus we have frequent accounts of the dying or anesthetized people while physically in a deep coma seeing their own bodies from a vantage point near the ceiling of the hospital room, hearing the conversation of those in the room, or even beginning a journey into another realm, only to be called back to this life.

After death, within a period of perhaps several hours, the etheric double dissolves, for it cannot long sustain separate existence without the physical body. The individual is then left with the astral body and the higher components, just as long ago on the third globe it had no more than these vehicles. This state is sometimes called Kamaloka, pleasure or desire world, or perhaps better the feeling-oriented world. It may more simply just be called life on the astral plane.

While astral life is real to the experiencer, it cannot be localized in terms of our material world. As H.P. Blavatsky said, "It has neither a definite area nor boundary, but exists *within* subjective space; i.e., is beyond our sensuous perceptions. Still it exists, and it is there that the astral *eidolons* [images or archetypes] of all the beings that have lived, animals included, await their *second death*" (*Key*, p. 143). It has been described as interpenetrating the physical world at every point, so that it exists in and around us.

On the astral plane the desires within the surviving self work themselves out until exhausted. It is said that a person who was much attached to the material things of this world may find the astral plane a purgatory or hell, since he will suffer excruciating desires which now cannot be fulfilled. Bereft of a physical body, his angers and hungers can only bubble in frustration until their energy finally subsides. (Some say that such an entity may try to fulfill such compulsions vicariously through other persons still in the flesh.)

A person whose grosser desires were more contained and whose emotional delights were more aesthetic or interpersonal, however, would find the astral plane a time of rest and growth and delight. Indeed, for all it is a period of purification, for without material objects the lower emotional energies gradually run down even in the crudest person, allowing relatively finer ones to develop.

The astral plane is sometimes referred to by the old Spiritualist term Summerland, and insofar as this suggests a state at once restful and zestful, it is not inappropriate. For though it has a few odd nooks and corners and some strange denizens, the astral plane can give rise to great joy and creativity. Its purpose in the pilgrimage is to help the Pilgrim disassociate from a desire nature linked to a particular physical world experience in order to continue the pilgrimage in another time, place, and physical vehicle.

The time spent in the Summerland may vary, depending on the intensity of the attachment. Some "earthbound" entities may linger long on the lowest astral levels near familiar haunts; stories of ghosts may be based on clairvoyant perception of them. But there is no eternal punishment; eventually the low astral energies wear down in even the most hardened cases, and the entity rises to higher levels.

There the positive side of astral life appears. Once bondage to the physical world is let go, the entity may realize a fresh and wonderful freedom. For the astral is a world of material marvelously plastic and subject to thought in a way far beyond the possibilities of hard matter. It easily becomes what one wants it to be. While some may make desire-objects which then enslave, the truly creative person will find mind-expanding scope to construct out of mind and feeling, art and fantasy realms which we on the physical plane can know only in dream and imagination.

Deep interpersonal love flourishes too, both within the plane and between its dwellers and those still in this world, for love chords with the highest of astral vibrations. It is said that loved ones in the astral visit those left behind especially in dreams, though they may also appear in visions or even, nowadays, send telephone calls, according to reports. (See Scott Rogo and Raymond Bayless. *Phone Calls from the Dead.* Prentice-Hall, 1979.)

Some clairvoyants have said that the stay on the astral plane lasts an average of twenty to forty years, though much shorter and much longer periods can occur, depending on the spiritual state of the individual at the time of death. Special problems are presented in death by violence, sudden accident, suicide, capital punishment, and in childhood; these have been discussed by theosophical writers. They unanimously agree that loving prayer and meditation, as free as may be from depressed thoughts, on the part of the living greatly assist the departed to make their adjustment to astral life and to transit it quickly.

For when the astral energies have been exhausted and their lessons assimilated, the entity falls into a sleep which is what Blavatsky referred to as the "second death." The astral sheath falls away and dissolves, and the entity then awakens to an even greater life, life in heaven or what theosophy calls Devachan.

After the physical, etheric, and astral sheaths have been left behind, what is left is the divine Trinity within, plus the intuitional and mental vehicles. The mental and intuitional are irradiated, as it were, from within by the Trinity. Near to its unimpeded warmth, and without pulls from physical sluggishness and astral desires however refined, mind and intuition find deep yet creative relaxation. Life in Devachan is mental life, but mental life on a very high level. It has two purposes: rest between incarnations, and assimilation of the experiences of the past life on a level that can be carried over to the next.

Here the mind can create worlds based on the thoughts and aspirations generated by the past life in order fully to understand and explore them. These will be one's highest, least selfish ideas, for thoughts related to the desire-levels will have already fallen away. If all goes well, the mental creations of Devachan will provide the ultimate basis for creativity in the physical world of one's next incarnation.

We can and do, then, create our own Heaven. But it will be no better than what we bring to it—bubbly or subtle joy, ecstasy, or that still peace which is deeper than any fervor, form-filled or transcending all form.

Eventually, all the thought-seeds brought into Devachan will be exhausted, rest and detachment from the last life will have run its course, and the entity will begin to desire new experience to add to what has gone before and now been assimilated. It is time for a new birth in a new physical, astral, and lower mental encasement. The stream of karma rises even to Devachan and lifts the Pilgrim back into the course of this (or another) world, where it will find a womb prepared. Greatly advanced souls may be able to help make a conscious choice concerning the next birth, but most will be simply impelled by the karma they have generated in lives now consciously forgotten. What they carry over is not actual memories, no more than an actual body, but a mental nature whose style, character, and seed-potentialities have been shaped through the long incubation of Devachan. From these come a new unique person subtly related to one now far in the past—and who has certain karmic debts to pay and issues to resolve.

People ask if you are going to heaven or hell. Theosophists say that we have all been in both countless
times, to the extent necessary, as we make our own
astral environment by the thoughts and feelings we
generate. We will probably be in both innumerable
time again, though we may call heaven and hell by
other names if we wish. For embodied life is a long,
long process of manifestation and withdrawal.

It should be added that an increasing number of
theosophical thinkers now suggest that many, perhaps the great majority, of persons do not pass
through the entire astral and Devachan experience
after each lifetime, but may reincarnate rather quickly with little process of transformation on the inner
planes between lives. This might be particularly the
case with those who die physically after only a relatively brief lifetime. It helps to explain those who
come with apparent memories of previous lives, and
with strong unresolved issues churning inside them,
or loves or beliefs so potent as to seem inexplicable
solely in terms of the present life.

We might ask why we need to go through the
traumas of birth and death at all. Could not nature be
programmed so that an organism could simply
regenerate itself over and over, without death at least
so long as the universe lasts? Perhaps. But it would
not then be serving, as physical life must, the higher
purposes of life, to enable the Pilgrim's infinite
journey through space and time to the One. That requires that we experience, and then withdraw—to
learn *how* to withdraw, and to know *what* we have
experienced, in all its ramifications and potential for
the future. To learn we must do it, over and over, till
finally we move on to other experiences and eventually drop all that is finite.

Theosophy has occasionally been accused of denigrating the physical world and physical body, as though to say one should put these down in favor of a more "spiritual" existence. But this is based on misunderstanding. Theosophy emphasizes that all reality as we know it is the interaction of spirit and matter. Theosophists strongly affirm all aspects of physical existence which are nonselfish and do not impede awareness of all dimensions of reality, both material and spiritual. They have vigorously affirmed the beauty of nature and art and the wonder of childhood and human love. The whole point of our present life in the fourth globe and Fifth Race is to experience and know the meaning of the physical, "dense-matter" plane; to refuse that task would be to refuse a necessary step in evolution in the Great Plan. Just as in the biological world, progress and newness are achieved through dropping outmoded forms, so in the course of human experience we need new bodies over and over to meet new challenges to be explored.

Rather, theosophy suggests only that there is more than separate physical existence as we here know it, and that the physical has no meaning without that more. Life and death themselves sound the same message—we are to experience but not to hold. Yet the physical body for us is the receptacle of the "more," of all the human sheaths or principles. As Buddhism also tells us, full enlightenment comes to us rarely in heaven or anywhere else beyond, almost always in a physical body on earth. Here in this world of day and night, good and evil, the Pilgrim faces challenges in their fullness; here the full armory is ready to confront them; here they must be mastered in flesh and blood reality.

PHENOMENA FROM THE INNER PLANES

The discussion of life and death and the constituents of human nature have left some "picking up" to do. Here is a brief catalog of several topics which should be mentioned, as the reader may come across them in other theosophical literature.

Astral Shell. Sometimes it seems that the astral sheath of an individual, or part of it, does not completely disintegrate after the "second death" when the entity drops it. It may retain a dim life of its own as an "astral shell" for a time, guided by mindless emotion, sometimes attaching itself parasitically to a congenial living host. The shells are said to account for some ghost stories, and also, drawn as a parasite to the aura of a medium, to be the basis of much spiritualistic phenomena; Blavatsky liked to emphasize that the usual communicator in seances is not the real *mind* of the deceased but such a lower remnant.

Aura. Clairvoyants often report an ability to see radiances or patterns of light around persons. The color and texture give clues to the state of consciousness, and the physical and spiritual health, of the individual. According to theosophy, auras may be made up of a complex combination of etheric, astral, and mental matter which the clairvoyant is able to perceive, although the most significant ones originate on the border of the mental and astral planes, where the activity of the former is reflected in the configurations of astral matter. When comparable patterns appear as a "cloud" above or near a person, they may be called "thought-forms," and as such have been reported in theosophical literature.

Deva. The Hindu word for god, especially a naturegod. In theosophy this term has been used to refer to

entities of mental and/or astral material who rule
nature and guide natural evolution. They range from
mighty beings enthroned over great mountains or
seascapes to tiny elfin creatures who may be the
spirit of a single flower. Some, though not all,
theosophical thinkers consider them as on a separate
line of evolution from animals and humans. They
have been vividly described by such theosophical
clairvoyants as Geoffrey Hodson.

Elementals. In much occult literature, this term refers to spirits like the devas who are associated with
the traditional four elements: earth, air, fire, and
water. The word has also been used incorrectly in
the same sense as "astral shells."

Chakras. From the Sanskrit meaning "wheel," this
term refers to subtle centers of psychospiritual
energy in the body known to esoteric yoga. Seven in
number, they interpenetrate the spinal column between its base and the top of the skull; as the *kun-
dalini,* a powerful psychic force, is aroused through
yoga and raised up the spine and through a subtle
nervous system, it successively "opens" these
centers to facilitate new psychic energies and finally
cosmic consciousness. Theosophical writers like C.
W. Leadbeater have adapted and modified somewhat
the chakra concept, speaking of them as vortices in
the etheric double as well as at the astral and mental
levels.

Latent Powers. The last of the three objectives of
the Theosophical Society includes investigating "the
powers latent in man." This means first of all spiritual wisdom and compassion, and spiritual will or in-
tentionality able to give direction to life, together
with ability to integrate one's physical and subtle
fields.

In a more restricted sense, the term may also allude to powers of clairvoyance and of utilizing healing energies. Clairvoyance, already mentioned, means "clear seeing" of that which is normally invisible; clairvoyants are those able to perceive auras, thought-forms, and entities of etheric, astral, or mental "stuff," and so to give us information about those planes.

Paranormal healers utilize subtle energies to channel healing force—usually through the etheric and taking advantage of its close interaction with the physical body—to heal those afflicted in mind or body. This is a vast subject I can only mention here. Suffice it to note that theosophists, while not endorsing all claims to clairvoyance or paranormal healing, tend to find the matter of interest and that its basic premises are not inconsistent with their view of reality.

4
On the Path

Fundamental to theosophy is a sense that human life (and that of all sentient beings) is impelled to move in the direction of fuller being and greater wisdom and joy. This means that, when it is most true to its real nature, life seeks those experiences which most open it to the Trinity within and to the divine in the cosmos. Such experiences, as we have seen, may be called expansions of consciousness or initiations; like any occasion of deep learning, they may be difficult, but they force fresh and widening ranges of perception.

If initiations are available, so must also be a path through them. Merely haphazard, disconnected awakenings could be of only limited value and might in fact confuse if not destroy. Many are the inmates of institutions for the mentally ill who have had visions of hidden realities which were perhaps valid, but for which neither they nor their society were prepared.

118

It is also true that certain persons seem to have a radiance and an inner power which sets them apart, making them unforgettable to all who meet them. They are the saints and God-realized of all religions. Often tales are told of their miraculous works; if sometimes these may be only pious legend, still their existence undoubtedly testifies to a well-founded human awareness that spiritual awakening can afford intuitive insight into "the hidden side of things."

We say, "He or she is where I would like to be," and we sense usually that the holy one has successfully managed an arduous inner journey, ending up not mad but supremely sane. That means the saint set out on pilgrimage with the right steps, and the initiations were traversed in the right sequence.

There is, in other words, a path—a right way to go about the development of the inner dimensions of a human being of which we have already spoken. This path is parallel to the group evolution of races and worlds presented in previous chapters, but is individual. The individual has his or her own potential for development and need not walk in lockstep with the rest. He can move far ahead—or lag far behind.

In either case, the advancing or lagging individual has an interaction with the rest of humanity. A human being can never truly exist singly. On overt or subtle levels, he is linked to the destiny of the human race as a whole. The person far in advance spiritually is there precisely because he or she has learned great compassion and displayed great capacity for self-less service, so now it is natural for that person to guide the forward movement of others, indeed of the world.

He is what is known in theosophy as a Master, an Adept, or Mahatma. Even if the time comes when his calling is no longer associated with this particular world, he is great because he lives for that which is greater than himself, though it may be on planes beyond our understanding.

To put it another way, utilizing the Eastern and theosophical concept of karma, each of us is basically impelled by our own karma, and so by the diligence with which we deal with our own karmic tasks. But we are also affected by group karma, the karmic webs woven by our various communities collectively, and we must deal with them as well until we reach the point of being able to influence such entire patterns of karma for good. A Master has transcended the realms of ordinary karma and can go some ways to take on and straighten out the group karmas with which he is involved, as he can also the karmas of disciples, rather than being simply subject to them.

How does one set foot on the great path? First, let me suggest that its twin pillars are wisdom and compassion. (This is the terminology of Mahayana Buddhism, but the same essential concept can be found in most spiritual traditions.) The path, then, rests on knowing and doing; it is a process of growing in wisdom and love expressed in action. The twin supports of these are meditation and service, underwritten by study and effort.

The wisdom upon which the path depends is not simply verbal knowledge about philosophical truths, however profound. All words are relative and we must go beyond them. True wisdom is rather *prajna,* in the Sanskrit term, or *prajnaparamita,* "the wisdom that has gone beyond." It is awareness greater than words, awareness which begins with awareness of one's own true nature as one with the true nature of the universe in which we are embedded—an awareness which comes by meditation, stilling the outer layers of consciousness so that the innermost can shine forth with its own light.

Meditation should be accompanied by study, for though even the wisest and most exalted thoughts should not intrude upon meditation proper, they help subtly prepare the mind for it and to release its influence into the rest of one's life. Further, the mind as *manas* is meant to be used as a vehicle of creativity and experience and not *only* to be "gone beyond"— as a vehicle it needs the fuel of the best thoughts.

Service is equally essential. By service is meant work in the world which advances evolution in the right direction. It is work which helps all sentient beings, and humanity as a whole, on the way back through the globes to ultimate reunion with the One. It means, therefore, service grounded in compassion or love, for love is no more and no less than the ethical expression of oneness, the final truth realized by wisdom.

Compassion, "feeling with," or love is action based on recognition of the oneness of my life with another's, that what the other suffers I must suffer, and that what I do for the other I do for myself, since our lives are bound together and share the same divine nature. Any action based on anything less than that realization retains some trace, large or small, of egocentricity, and hence to that extent is founded neither on compassion nor on wisdom.

For wisdom and compassion are utterly inseparable; we cannot truly have one without the other. Any supposed wisdom that does not express itself in compassionate behavior is false, no wisdom at all—in the words of St Paul, "sounding brass or a tinkling cymbal." Compassion without wisdom, on the other hand, is perhaps not to be so roundly con-

demned, since it is incumbent upon us to do what we
can to ease the suffering of the world and to live well
with others, even though we may still "see in a glass
darkly" regarding all ends and means thereof. Yet
compassion alone may be less effective than it ought
to be, for without the clear eye of wisdom cleansed in
selfless study and meditation, we are likely to retain
too much of ego. We are in imminent danger of confusing the service to others with imposing our own
will on them, with making them dependent and enjoying their gratitude, and of falling into gross or
subtle states of self-congratulation. One can only
advance in the path by growth in wisdom and compassion together, profoundly interconnected.

The classic theosophical books continually emphasize the importance of duty and service. Sometimes to our jaded modern ears they may sound a bit
preachy on the subject, but the emphasis is absolutely crucial. Today's "pop" spirituality often seems so
busy seeing it all as a cosmic joke, or going beyond
all such "hangups" as conscience, or doing anything
other than what feels good at the moment, that it has
little time to hear the cries of the hungry, the tor-
tured, the abused children, or the tormented animals
in their millions over this planet.

Such "spirituality" is utterly false and must be de-
nounced outright. One can no more know oneself or
the oneness of all things without knowing the
anguish of myriads who are part of that web of life,
and responding to their anguish as though to one's
own, than one could act in a play and ignore all the
other actors in their parts. Theosophy with its sober
stress on duty and service provides a very important
corrective to the cheap (and empty) bliss of those
grossly foreshortened "paths."

One's way of duty (or dharma) and service, though, is one's own, determined by one's karma, personality, and inner potentials. If all persons were to interpret service in exactly the same way, the world would not work; on the other hand, if each were to follow one's own way fully, the world would mesh together like a great dance and all would be well, for on the deepest levels there is harmony amid all individual tendencies.

Service may be physical, social, or spiritual. For some, like Albert Schweitzer or Mother Teresa, it may mean going far from home to minister to the sick and dying. For others, it may mean doing much —perhaps very quietly—where one is. Some may be called mainly to work devotedly for the Theosophical Society, or some other good cause. Some may be mainly teachers of the Way.

Some may find that their calling to service can be mainly fulfilled within their vocation—and not only if they are in an obviously service-oriented profession, such as that of nurse or social worker. To be a thoroughly dedicated, conscientious artist, or house painter, is equally service. Yet one must examine oneself very deeply in these matters to be sure one is doing *all* one is called to do, and not using one calling as an excuse to avoid another, perhaps less pleasant, form of service one knows needs to be done.

That short and beautiful theosophical classic, *At the Feet of the Master*, sums it up well:

> Four qualifications there are for this pathway:
>> Discrimination
>> Desirelessness
>> Good Conduct
>> Love

Stages Along the Way

Where exactly does this path lead?

Even to suggest particular steps has its dangers. First, each individual's experience of the path is different. Although some standard accounts present stages on the road to enlightenment, such as those which will be offered here, others combine or divide certain ones.

More significantly, different seekers will traverse the way differently. A study of the lives of major spiritual masters will reveal that some have seemingly skipped one or more stages, or experienced two or more simultaneously, or attained great holiness without proceeding through the whole course but doing only one or two simple spiritual tasks exceedingly well. It would be a great travesty if something as subtle and personal as the spiritual life were viewed as some sort of automatic assembly-line process which one enters at one end and comes out the other a certified saint!

For the masters, it has always been far more a matter of art than technique; while they may have particular methods of prayer, meditation, or yoga to impart, these are at best like the stylistic practices of a great writer or painter. Unless combined with the devotion and insight of the master, the techniques will not produce the same end. Furthermore, it is well known that the greatest artists have their good and bad days, their moments of ecstasy and despair. So it is with the saints; no spiritual automatic pilot will suspend their human variety, nor should it.

Nevertheless, just as a road map can be of aid to one making a journey, so can a schematic of the spiritual path assist in the vast enterprise of growth into Eternity. To be sure, different travelers following the same map and endeavoring to journey between the same two points may have quite different adventures. One may make an easy drive on a bright sunny day, another get caught in a downpour; one have a flat tire or even a collision involving long delays, and another get lost despite the map and wander around the countryside for a while. But the map is still of value for two reasons: first, it reminds us, regardless of appearances, that there is a road and it has been traveled successfully by others; second, it points out at least some of the landmarks along the way, even if it cannot account for every vicissitude. In the same way, an outline of the spiritual path can reassure us, in the moments of deep doubt and despair that are bound to come, that people before have moved through such dark times to ultimate victory; and it can suggest some, if not all, of the fields and high passes we may be plodding through.

Here, then, is an outline of the spiritual way. The five stages to be listed are based on those in Evelyn Underhill's classic work, *Mysticism*. They will then be compared with the stages of initiation given in the theosophical work *The Masters and the Path* by C. W. Leadbeater.

1. *Awakening of the Soul.* First one must be drawn to the path. Sometimes the call is simply a steady deepening of spiritual interest based on early training and augmented by study and reflection. It may be so gradual that one cannot say precisely that the path "started" at one time or another. Again, one may be led to "something more" by a progressive or sudden despair at the emptiness of the ordinary life. On the other hand, there are those who report a distinct "summons" or an overpowering conversion experience. In any case, something snaps the hold of

purely material values and leads one, perhaps stumbling and half-blinded by new light at first, toward other realms.

The awakening stage is exciting but not without its dangers and temptations. Beginning spiritual experiences are likely to be highly emotional and so forceful as to lead one to absolutize whatever the religious and ideological context in which they came. One is tempted to hold to the rich emotional feelings they release and be despondent when, as with all emotional moods, they fade away; one is also easily seduced into thinking that, after such impressive blessings, one now "has it all" instead of realizing that even the greatest awakening experience usually does little more than open the door a crack; the great journey has barely begun.

Purgation or Preparation. The stabilization of the spiritual path for the long haul is the task of the next stage. This is a time when the careful following of a spiritual discipline—regular prayer, meditation, yoga, or whatever it is—is important in order to dig straight channels for the emotional/spiritual tides aroused by the awakening. Otherwise, one may be lost amid tumultuously shifting moods and feelings. It is also important to bring one's entire life style into harmony with the spiritual practice, or else the schism between the two may be greater than one's frame can safely bear.

The Illuminative Way. After a time, the discipline bears fruit. One enters a period of wonderful religious fulfillment. Prayers are answered and the presence of God is deeply felt. One knows hours of spiritual joy, and the truth taught by one's tradition seems profoundly meaningful. For many this stage is what spirituality is all about and is enough.

Yet even now problems remain. One can be subtly attached to God and to prayer or meditation as others are to the pleasures of the table or the bottle. So long as one thinks of God as another to whom one prays, or of times of prayer and meditation, however rewarding, as being special and apart, one implies there is that which is other than God and times when God is less present. For certain souls, a second and deeper purgation will strike at even these remaining impediments to full union with God or Ultimate Reality.

The Dark Night of the Soul. This stage was given its best-known description by the Spanish saint, John of the Cross. At this point the wellsprings of prayer and meditation seem to run dry, and one is as though lost on a desert at midnight without a compass. One feels betrayed, abandoned by the God in whom one trusted. Many give way to doubt and despair. Yet those who persevere through this season of testing come to realize that in it a very profound process of purification has taken place. It prepares one to know God within, rather than as another, deeper than words or feelings, and to sense him in an inner stillness which is greater than any rapture.

The Unitive State. The seeker is then ready for the ultimate stage, which goes by many names throughout the world: salvation, liberation, enlightenment, union with God. Its sovereign characteristic seems to be that it is perceived as a condition of full freedom, without boundaries, for one is so profoundly oned with God that even if, in the words of the Psalmist, one can be cast down to hell, God is there also. It is therefore the Zen "Gateless Gate," the "darkness and waylessness" of the Christian mystic Jan de Ruysbroeck, where the only guide is love, and external compasses are of no more use than they would be if the entire country were turned into the magnetic pole.

One is now wholly freed for a life of selfless, compassionate service. The great saints and masters most deeply involved in the welfare of the world are at this stage. Not a few of them, after a period of intense, enclosed spiritual practice, have gone forth into the world to love and serve, now so inwardly united to God they no longer need be hampered by obligations of time and place. They know God beyond words at all times and places, in fountain, flower, and the faces of the suffering, and while they do not disdain formal prayer, neither are they in bondage to forms for inwardly they "pray without ceasing."

An archetype of such a person is seen in the last of the famous Zen "Ox Herding Pictures." Here the seeker, after an arduous quest for the true self symbolized by a lost ox, emerges victorious to enter the city "with bliss-bearing hands." He is shown proceeding down the road, an immense grin on his face, laughing, dancing, and playing with children, utterly unselfconscious or constrained, freely giving joy to all high and low.

The Path of the Masters

Let us now turn to the way as presented in Leadbeater's *The Masters and the Path*.* A quite similar outline can be found by comparing his view of "the way of the Master" and the initiations with Underhill's,

---

* C.W. Leadbeater, *The Masters and the Path*. Adyar, Madras, India; Theosophical Publishing House, 1925, 1965. Page numbers after citations.

save that Leadbeater, in accordance with his school
of theosophy, sees the progress as being made under
the tutelage of some particular "Master of Wisdom"
of whom the student is a protege.

Leadbeater does not give an account of inward
awakening experiences as such. But he does implic-
itly tell us how one may come to them:

> There are always the three ways: a man may bring
> himself to the Master's feet by deep study, because
> in that way he comes to know and to feel; and cer-
> tainly He may be reached by deep devotion long
> continued, by the constant uplifting of the soul
> towards Him. And there is also the method of
> throwing oneself into some definitive activity for
> Him. (p. 55)

These three ways, which correspond to the jnana-
yoga, bhakti-yoga, and karma-yoga of Hinduism, suggest that any profound involvement in the things of
the spirit—whether in study, devotion to one's
deities, or selfless work—will awaken one to the path
and set one's foot upon it, through a relationship
with those already far advanced in that great
pilgrimage.

Elsewhere, Leadbeater looks at it from a different
angle:

> There are two ways in which people are led to the
> Path—by reading and hearing of it, and by being
> in close association with those who are already
> treading it. The third way which is mentioned in
> Oriental books is by intellectual development; by
> sheer force of hard thinking a man may come to
> grasp some of these principles, though I think that
> method is rare. Again, they tell of a fourth way—
> that by the long practice of virtue men may come
> to the beginning of the Path—that a man may so
> develop the soul by steadily practicing the right so

> far as he knows it that eventually more and more
> of the light will open before him. (p. 135)

Though differently put, these ways of being led
toward the path are certainly not inconsistent with
the three already cited. The underlying principle is
clear. By involving oneself with what goes *with* the
path—ideas appropriate to it, people already on it,
works like those of the saints walking it—one will
find that path in the more formal sense. For like
seeks like, good karma engenders more of the same,
and the Masters on their part seek those ready for
them.

Clearly, this seeking may be a conscious or uncon-
scious quest. If one knows of the existence of the
path and intentionally wants to get on it, the thing
to do is to act in accordance with it. Sooner or later
the inward awakening will come, or in Leadbeater's
terms a Master will accept the seeker as a disciple
and lead him up the path in a formal sense. But it is
just as true that, though one be ignorant of the
Masters and the path, if one nonetheless studies and
serves for the sake of learning and love alone, that
person is just as surely on the great path.

For Leadbeater, the first stage is Probation, a
period closely related to the Purgative or Preparatory
Way of Underhill. It is a time for work, vigilance, and
discipline. With a characteristic theosophic emphasis, Leadbeater stresses the importance of service. In
the chapter on Probation, he quotes a Master:

> I know that your one object in life is to serve the
> Brotherhood; yet do not forget that there are
> higher steps before you, and that progress on the
> Path means sleepless vigilance. You must not only
> be always *ready* to serve; you must be ever watch-
> ing for opportunities—nay, *making* opportunities
> to be helpful in small things, in order that when

the greater work comes you may not fail to see it.
(p. 81)

The Illuminative stage clearly corresponds with what Leadbeater speaks of as the first, second, and third formal initiations. Through them and the course of development each represents, one overcomes the "three fetters"—delusion of self, doubt or uncertainty, and superstition (p. 201)—and acquires occult power to utilize the subtle bodies.

These several tasks and levels are similar to Evelyn Underhill's remarks on the pluralism of the Illuminative stage, its "ways within the Way." We also sense that it is a level of joy and love as well as zestful effort, with probation behind one. Leadbeater puts stress on the deepening love between the Master and the disciple at this point, as each gives up self for the other and the great work: "Yet this utter sacrifice, this utmost resignation of the self brings with it a keener joy than aught else on earth can confer, for such love alone is god-like, such self-surrender bears the man into the very heart of Christ." (p. 180).

It is the subsequent fourth initiation, however, which most vividly reveals the parallel between Leadbeater's scenario and Underhill's, for it is a striking equivalent to the Dark Night of the Soul. The fourth initiation is explicitly compared to the crucifixion and resurrection of Christ. Its most impressive feature is the experience of total aloneness that the initiate must undergo:

> It is one of the features of the fourth initiation that the man shall be left entirely alone. First he has to stand alone on the physical plane; all his friends turn against him through some misunderstanding; it all comes right afterwards but for the time the man is left with the feeling that all the world is against him.

Perhaps that is not so great a trial, but there is another and inner side to it; for he has also to experience for a moment the condition called Avichi, which means "the waveless," that which is without vibration. The state of Avichi is not, as has been popularly supposed, some kind of hell, but it is a condition in which the man stands absolutely alone in space, and feels cut off from all life, even from that of the Logos; and it is without doubt the most ghastly experience that it is possible for any human being to have. It is said to last only for a moment, but to those who have felt its supreme horror it seemed an eternity, for at that level time and space do not exist. (p. 220)

After this desolation comes a breakthrough into the supreme state, equivalent to the Unitive and here called Nirvana: "The entry into it is utterly bewildering, and it brings as its first sensation an intense vividness of life, surprising even to him who is familiar with the buddhic plane" (p. 223). The theme of unity is central to it:

The man who has once realized that marvelous unity can never forget it, can never be quite as he was before; for however deeply he may veil himself in lower vehicles in order to help and save others, however closely he may be bound to the cross of matter, cribbed, cabined and confined, he can never forget that his eyes have seen the King in His Beauty, that he has beheld the land which is very far off—very far off, yet very near, within us all the time if we could only see it, because to reach Nirvana we need not go away to some far-distant heaven, but only open our consciousness to its glory (p. 229).

THE MASTERS

We now come to the role of those who have passed through those higher initiations and advanced far along the great path. Theosophists most commonly call them Masters, Adepts, or Mahatmas (the Hindu term for "Great Soul"). They have also been referred to as the Elder Brothers of the race.

Like so much of theosophical terminology, such words are only pointers. For some people today they may sound excessively antiquated, authoritarian, or masculine. Other words could be, and have been, substituted: Helpers, Friends, Wise Ones, Knowers.

The point is that theosophists teach that some persons have definitely progressed well ahead of the bulk of the human race and are committed to helping the rest of us. This is no strange or peculiar doctrine, for almost all religions have their saints, bodhisattvas, immortals, or God-realized ones in a similar role. The main difference is that, for theosophy, these advanced ones are drawn from all religions and all parts of the globe to form a Brotherhood which invisibly aids the world, including from time to time starting religions to meet the needs of diverse peoples and cultures. For the great path is limited to no one faith or society, but may commence in any of these and proceed to the mountaintop where all converge.

Theosophists also emphasize that at least some Masters—if we may continue to use the most common term—are on this earth in physical bodies. They are not overseeing things from a distant heaven or some disembodied mode of existence. Rather, it is said they are among us here on earth. Some, like the living saints of all faiths, may be walking the streets of our great cities or countrysides. More typically, according to the classic theosophical sources, they live in retirement in remote places like Tibet or Mongolia, where their contemplation and work for good on the inner planes can be uninterrupted.

However, again like the saints or bodhisattvas of

all faiths, their advanced spiritual state gives them mastery of little-known laws of nature, the so-called "mayavic" powers or control of appearances. Such powers enable them to appear in different forms anywhere in the world, to communicate by telepathy or the "precipitation" of messages on paper, and to work seeming miracles at a distance. Certain Masters, it is said, prefer to dwell in their astral or mental bodies only, affording greater freedom but less contact with the physical human experience they have gone beyond.

In any case, the Masters' supreme imperatives are wisdom and compassion. The "mayavic" powers are a direct result of wisdom, or seeing things as they really are, in all their interrelatedness. Such knowledge, unclouded by ignorance or illusion, includes perceiving the subtle forces which make the world appear as it does, and also includes awareness of what could influence or "bend" those forces to alter appearances, including one's own form.

But one who *has* awesome wisdom, who could wield such mighty levers, could ultimately do so only out of compassion, for to act with any lesser motive is to allow the fog of illusion again to move before one's eyes. (However, it is possible to gain considerable occult power over appearances on the basis of skill only, without wisdom or compassion, as might a black magician. In the end, though, the emptiness of such pretense must be shown up.) Many members of the Theosophical Society feel that the Masters whom the founders of the movement knew, though not necessarily infallible, were and are possessed of a very high wisdom and compassion and may be trusted as guides in the Ancient Wisdom and the evolution of self and world.

A related idea in theosophy is that of the *chela* or disciple. According to Leadbeater, one setting foot on the path of discipleship may be accepted by a Master as a student and gains an increasingly warm and close relationship to that exalted one. This point should be mentioned, but it is not one of which much can be said here. For most theosophists the relationship would not take outward institutional form, as in the ashrams of ordinary gurus and their disciples. Rather, theosophists tend to consider the relationship, and the initiations it entails, to be inward. Such things are expressed in dreams, mystical experiences, and subtle communication on inner levels. Yet undoubtedly the trend of these inward adventures would parallel normal progress along the great path.

THE GREAT LODGE

One can find several titles for the fellowship of Masters in classic theosophical literature: the Elder Brethren, the Brotherhood of the Masters of the Wisdom, the Occult Brotherhood, the Universal Mystic Brotherhood.

All these titles grow somewhat out of the cultural milieu of those pioneers of modern theosophy who received intimations of the existence of the Masters. In particular, such designations borrow from the model of Freemasonry and the ancient and medieval mystery lodges which lie behind it. These are built on the model of a lodge or brotherhood into which one is initiated after receiving certain information and making certain solemn commitments, and within which one can similarly advance to higher and higher "degrees." We must emphasize that this model is only a model, that is, it is *our* way of understanding a reality that may look different from other perspectives. Yet this model does undoubtedly fit basic facts about the Masters, as indeed it does all of life. Life and growth are a series of initiations, they demand commitment to wisdom and compassionate service, and those who have experienced such initiations and share such commitments enjoy a unique fellowship one with another. But the plurality of terms for that fellowship, and for those adepts, itself shows us that no particular words are mandated.

Many theosophists from Blavatsky on have tried to describe the Masters, their names, ranks, duties, and way of life. Yet these accounts are beyond independent verification. In the end the Brotherhood remains real but elusive.

It is real for many theosophists basically for two reasons, which may be spoken of as arguments from experience and congruity. The first argument simply takes note of the fact that persons in whom theosophists have found an unusual portion of wisdom and stature, beginning with the founders of modern theosophy, Helena Blavatsky and Henry Steel Olcott, have acknowledged ongoing personal contact with the Masters. The argument from congruity is the observation that the existence of such a hierarchy fits the evolutionary and subtle-planes view of reality so well it would be surprising if beings in advance of the majority did not exist.

Yet the Masters remain beings we are not prepared fully to comprehend, for their very state of understanding, their wisdom and compassion blending with the interrelatedness of all things, makes them more "part of the background" than we. It is egotism like ours which makes an entity stick out in the world; those who have gone far to vanquish ego work with quiet and unobtrusive effectiveness. Like the ideal ruler described in the *Tao Teh Ching*, they lead without anyone knowing it, so that people say, "We did this ourselves."

The Masters may well meet us at the growth-parameters of our lives, guiding those of us open to growth through dreams, seemingly accidental or co-incidental occurrences they control through "maya-vic" powers, even encountering us at the right times in the guise of mysterious "chance" meetings. Yet they will not "pull rank" or impose themselves, for they know full well that they cannot arrogate another's life to themselves or force another's growth. Spiritual growth is a subtle thing, requiring on the one hand humility and due acknowledgment of the grace or spiritual energies of the universe without which one can do nothing, and on the other hand individual effort and responsibility. Such growth can be stimulated, nourished, and guided from without but not compelled, just as one can plant and water a vine and lead its tendrils onto trellises, but the growth itself must come from within.

Henry Olcott put it well in *Old Diary Leaves* when he said of the the Masters' work:

> Unseen, unsuspected as the vivifying spiritual currents of the Akash, yet as indispensable for the spiritual welfare of mankind, their combined divine energy is maintained from age to age and forever refreshes the pilgrim of Earth, who struggles on towards the Divine Reality (I:18).

Though much is unknown, theosophical literature has provided us with the names or titles and work of some of the Masters. While certainly not dogma, this material is interesting and a summary of some of it may be of help to the reader of further theosophical literature.

First there is the Solar Logos, ruler of our solar system whose outward expression is the physical orb of the sun. This Being is far greater than the Masters associated with Earth and the history of the Theosophical Society; he is more like a divine entity who is the spiritual impulse behind our star and its far-flung family of planets. Yet his position is one to which he evolved over unimaginable aeons from a condition comparable to ours. He is said now to be, for all intents and purposes, like the conventional notion of God, expressing the divine Trinity of being, intellect, and mind or bliss in our sector of the universe with its innumerable souls.

Next come the Solar Pitris or Manasaputras, the "angels" or agents of the Solar Logos, "Sun-Fathers" or "Sons of Mind," bright, pure beings, wise in their own sphere. The most celebrated are, of course, those higher beings spoken of earlier called Lords of the Flame, who came to Earth in the Lemurian epoch, taking forms to guide the newly embodied protohumans in their slow progress toward full humanity. Some sources speak of their leader as Sanat Kumara, the "Eternal Youth," also called the "Lord of the Earth" and the "One Initiator," who thus becomes a sort of personification of the World-Soul, especially in its role as facilitator of spiritual aspiration.

Then there are the Masters with whom Helena P. Blavatsky was in close rapport, and first named by her, the Master Morya and the Master Kuthumi. They are said to reside in Tibet and to have been her initiators there; as her mentors, they were the real Founders of the Theosophical Society. As M. and K.H., they have attributed to them the famous "Mahatma Letters" to A.P. Sinnett.

Still another group of Masters is mentioned in early modern theosophical literature, particularly Series I of H.S. Olcott's *Old Diary Leaves*. They include a Copt, an Alexandrian Neo-Platonist, a Venetian, an English philosopher (p. 19), a Hungarian (p. 275), and seven members of the "Brotherhood of Luxor" (pp. 75-78). As we shall see, most of these reappear in the literature of the second generation of theosophical literature as the Masters of the Seven Rays.

A fourth set of Masters are those great, generally known spiritual teachers of humanity throughout the ages who, from the theosophical point of view, are in fact Masters engaged in public work. Their ranks included such exalted figures as the Buddha, Krishna, and Jesus.

At this point a word about Jesus as a Master may be in order. If we set aside for a moment the perspective of Christian dogmatics and just look at the life of Jesus as it is presented in the Gospels, we will see that it offers a beautiful paradigm of the role and inner career of a Master. Jesus was deeply immersed in one culture and religious tradition, the Judaic. Yet though he began with Moses and the prophets, he urged his listeners, believers like himself in that tradition, to explore its farthest frontiers in the ideal of the Kingdom of Heaven, yet also the present rule of God on earth as in Heaven. Jesus saw God's rule everywhere—in nature in the fall of a sparrow, in human behavior under the Law, reflected in one's deepest and most inward thoughts.

Jesus can be seen passing through the classic stages of the spiritual life; the Awakening when he heard the preaching of John; Purgation or Probation subsequently in the forty days in the desert; the Illuminative Way during the golden days of his ministry with its wonderful miracles and blessings; the Dark Night when he hung abandoned upon the cross; the Unitive state after the Resurrection, when his life seemed full of light and free from all boundaries as he appeared in the midst of his disciples, now here and now there, behind closed doors or by the shores of the lake at dawn.

We also notice in Jesus, as in all great Masters, a certain reticence, an unconcern with personal honor or status. He apparently did not claim for himself the titles "Messiah" or "Son of God"; they were given him by others, notably Peter when he said, "Thou art the Christ (Messiah), the Son of the Living God," and Jesus replied, "Get thee behind me Satan!" He ran away when they tried to make him king; nor, for that matter, did he like the titles Father or Master. Instead, we see in Jesus that willingness to be a "part of the background," a facilitator or helper who dies to himself that others may live, an elusive and mysterious presence who is here but briefly, leaving a memory which blesses all generations, then all too soon slips out of sight, carrying his high-trailed pilgrimage elsewhere.

THE HIERARCHY AND THE SEVEN RAYS

We now come to a model most developed by the second generation of modern theosophy. Many theosophists would regard it as speculative, but it has a certain beauty and power and has inspired some interesting works of art. We are speaking of a model of the hierarchy of the Masters by which they guide the world and, in a special way, those who become their disciples.

Fundamental components of this model are the

Seven Rays, analogous to the seven lamps of the Book of Revelation and the "seven ways to bliss" of *The Secret Doctrine*. All human history and all human temperaments, all ways to serve and all ways to joy, are viewed as manifestations of one or another of seven "rays" which channel divine energy into the life of the world. Further, each of the rays is associated with one or more of the Masters, who is an expression of it and also aids on inner planes its benign work in the world. Let us then look at the Seven Rays one by one.

The First Ray is the Ray of leadership and pertains to strength, and so controls wise government and social organization. At a very high level its exponent is said to be Sanat Kumara, the Manasaputra "Lord of the World." Below him is the Manu, the Hindu term for a primordial man and lawgiver who is the progenitor of each age of the world; in theosophy each of the Root Races has its Manu. Finally, the Master Morya works on this Ray.

The Second Ray is devoted to wisdom and teaching. As the First governs the social organization of the world, so the Second is especially attuned to its inner religious and spiritual development, expressing the second corner of the divine Trinity, wisdom and intellect, as the First Ray expresses being or will. The Second Ray is manifested on a high level by the Buddha and below him by the World Teacher and future Buddha, the exalted being known as the Christ. Just as each Root Race is founded by a Manu, so each culminates spiritually in the appearance of a Buddha and at the same time bears in its bosom a bodhisattva or coming Buddha, who will be the Buddha of the next race. On a lower level the Master Kuthumi works on this Ray.

The next five rays are all aspects of the third corner

of the divine Trinity, mind/bliss/activity. They are under an entity known as the Mahachohan, like a Prime Minister to the members of his Cabinet.

Of this set, the Third Ray is under the Master called the Venetian. Its keynotes are adaptability, and a subtle sense of timing and of interrelationships. Astrology rightly understood—as the science of the interconnectedness of all things in the universe, the movement of the stars in their courses and in the affairs of men—is under this Ray, as is the right understanding of history and its great cycles.

The Fourth Ray is under the Master Serapis, a Coptic or Egyptian Greek. It is concerned with beauty and harmony, which express themselves in art; many artists are pursuing spiritual development through their work along the path of which it is the guiding light.

The Fifth Ray, guided by the Master Hilarion, a Neo-Platonist, is concerned with accuracy of observation and so with science; it is the path of those whom science leads to ultimate truth.

The Sixth Ray is guided by the Master Jesus. In theosophical accounts a distinction is made between Jesus and the Christ, the initiate Jesus having been overshadowed in his last years by a greater being, the Christ who is World Teacher on the Second Ray. The Sixth Ray rules the devotional path, the path of saints, mystics, and devotees of all faiths. We have already looked at Jesus' sublime exemplification of the spiritual way.

The Seventh Ray is headed by the Comte de St Germain, a celebrated and mysterious eighteenth-century French occultist. He is also known as the Master Rakoczy, who is the aforementioned Hungarian adept, and is said to have appeared as a number of famous earlier savants, including Francis and Roger

Bacon. This Ray governs the role of ceremony in human life. All ritual, whether Confucian in the East, Vedic in India, or ecclesiastical or magical in the West, reminds us that such stylized behavior can transform the participant, enabling him or her to lose the ego-self and become something greater, an ideal whose role is being acted out as by a performer in a great dance. In the experience of many, ritual can also of itself release extraordinary energies. All this is under the Seventh Ray, and to augment its force for good some theosophists have engaged in benign ritual activity, such as that of Co-Masonry or the Liberal Catholic Church.

THE MASTERS AND HUMAN LIFE

These then are some basic features of the theosophical view of the Masters and their work. While some aspects of the picture may be speculative, certain principles abide.

First, spiritually evolved people, theosophy says, do have an inner role in the guidance of the world. This principle is by no means exclusive to theosophy. Most religions give hidden but wide powers to their saints and holy ones. Islamic mysticism, for example, speaks of "pivot saints" who may outwardly be but ordinary, unprepossessing people, yet whose inner work sustains the earth; should they fail, it would fall apart.

Second, for theosophy, however, these hidden leaders are cross-cultural and cross-religious. All lands and faiths have produced them, or been produced by them, and all have their roles in the development of the world which is under their guidance (though they are not omnipotent).

Third, individuals may become students or disciples of a particular Master. One may find "resonance" with or be particularly drawn to the personality or work of one or another of the Masters of which theosophy, or the religions of the world, speak. In such case, it is entirely appropriate to work toward developing an inner relationship with that Master.

Fourth, as the panorama of the Rays makes evident, the Masters in their labors for the earth and the universe are not concerned only with "religion" or "spirituality" in any narrow sense, but equally with government, history, art, and science. All these must combine to make the great chords of the human symphony and cause it to resound on higher and higher planes. The coming of the next Races, and finally of the next worlds, will require contributions from all areas of human life. All will go together to make a better and better humanity. The statesmen, artists, and scientists will have their parts, just as will the devotees and the ritualists—and the theosophical occultists. But, under the hidden Masters guiding the ascent of each, all must harmonize their work more and more rather than pursuing the separate, if not discordant, development so characteristic of today.

Last is the principle that all the Masters were once as we. In theosophy, gods and men (using the terms loosely) are not separate orders but interchangeable. What they are, we may become; what we are, they were. Thus is enacted in our inward experience the interconnectedness, the oneness, of the universe, and is embodied a hope stupendous beyond imagining. For there is no height of wonder and power we cannot—and will not—scale, if we forget ego, to serve and love and grow wise.

5
Theosophical Interpretations of Evil

THE NATURE OF EVIL

A valuable perspective on any worldview can be obtained from the way it handles the problem of evil—why flaws seem to appear in the fabric of the universe, why bad things happen to good people, why suffering and frustration occur at all.

Generally, the problem is put in this form in the West: If God is good, why does he permit evil? Could he not have made a universe in which it was not permitted? The existence of evil must mean either a) that God is good but not all-powerful, or b) that God is all-powerful but not entirely good. Either possibility would hardly be reassuring to fragile creatures like ourselves. The way theosophy deals with this conundrum, and with the entire problem of evil, provides invaluable insights into the nature of its worldview.

First let us examine the nature of evil in fuller detail. There is no avoiding the fundamental fact that

---

This chapter is based on, and extensively reproduces, an article of the same title by the author in *The Theosophist*, 104, 1 (October 1982), pp. 23-30.

evil exists in human experience, whether you interpret it as illusion or necessity or whatever. It gnaws like a cankerworm at our otherwise beautiful universe and leaves very little of it untouched.

Evil exists in innumerable forms and has a variety of immediate causes. Some evil stems from human choice, from those who rob, cheat, lie, torture, kill. Indeed, few of us have hands and hearts wholly clean of at least the milder human sins, or the desire to commit them. If nothing more, we are guilty of countless sins of omission—of failure to do all we could on all occasions to alleviate the suffering of man or beast and to spread healing love.

Suffering also exists, apparently, as a part of nature itself: the city leveled by earthquake, the child wasted by incurable disease, the helpless animal devoured by a predator.

All this we see, and we feel within that it should not be. We might define evil as that which we feel ought not to be, yet is. In the words of St Paul, it is the "mystery of iniquity"; in those of Jesus, "the abomination. . . standing where it ought not."

What ought not to be. . . it seems to me that, fundamentally, evil blocks or prevents something from being what it is or is meant to become in accordance with its intrinsic nature. It is that which prevents a living creature from completing its life-cycle, from passing through the normal processes of gestation, growth, maturity, and old age. On a deeper level, it cuts the creature off from enjoying the unbounded fullness of life which all living things desire and which lies behind their need to eat, rest, mate, and play.

That which arrests this cycle and destroys this fulfillment we call evil: the animal killed (as most are) before the natural end of its life, the soldier hardly more than a boy blown to pieces in war, the victims of Auschwitz, all those sent to the grave early by plague and famine. All these horrors and countless others, from the ordinary human point of view, deprive these lives of their total meaning. For we see a life as most fulfilled if its full potential is allowed expression before it is terminated.

As if that were not enough, evil has two more disturbing features. First, it challenges any view we may have that the universe is rational. It makes us wonder if it works by any coherent principles comprehensible to human intellect or compatible with human purposes. For certainly nothing appears less rational than a universe whose beauty and harmony are spoiled by the cruel suffering embedded in it, and which spawns living things wholesale of which few will complete the life-cycle programmed into their structures.

In the last analysis, nothing is more profoundly depressing than a suspicion—or conviction—that the universe in which we find ourselves is pointless and irrational to the core. In such a universe a relatively few good days would be about all any creature is likely to get, and anything bad, however heartless and senseless, could happen to anyone at any time. Yet evidence around us pointing in that direction is far from lacking. To fend off its terror, humans have constructed all sorts of philosophical battlements and strained mightily to see the world's rewards and punishments distributed more even-handedly than appears on the surface. The struggle against seeing universal moral unreason is far from won in the minds of many; dread of irrationality at the ultimate level must be considered among evil's deepest-cutting weapons.

Second, evil spreads its pall beyond those directly affected. We feel a natural empathy—or fear—when we see others afflicted. In proportion to our sensitivity, we feel pain, sorrow, and pity at the suffering of a fellow-creature. We may also experience anxiety to the point of anguish that the suffering may spread. As Dostoevsky powerfully showed in *The Brothers Karamazov*, the suffering of a single abused child anywhere forever destroys any illusion that all around us is wholly good on any level, or even that such suffering as exists is clearly deserved.

Finally, the self-perpetuating character of evil must be mentioned. No single outcropping of evil is sufficient unto itself, for each inevitably appears as a part of a great interlocking web in which natural and human evil are intertwined and in which the evil tends to spread out from its initial epicenter like a pestilence.

An earthquake does not only raze a city; it also brings in its wake fire, famine, and disease. These in turn may arouse in their victims such privation and rage as to stir them to theft, murder, and even war. A neglected child is more likely to neglect his or her own children than one well cared for. If one child throws a stone at a bird others may follow suit, though the cruel sport might not have occurred to them otherwise. It is well known that war systematically degrades many of those who take part in it, making them, out of fear and callousness, progressively capable of greater and greater acts of violence, lust, and sadism. The fighting man who starts out full of chivalrous ideals about the campaign is very likely, six months later, to live only for survival and the release of unbearable tension that comes from violence. He will shoot whatever moves, shrink at any noise, and kill his enemy by whatever means are at hand.

These indications give some hint of the extent of

the evil which infests our cosmos. How does theosophy interpret it?

Theosophy gives several answers to the problem. It suggests that not just one but several forces may be at work to create the evil we see around us. This in itself is significant, for it is what we should expect if evil is, in fact, fundamentally irrational, a reversion to chaos and meaninglessness. If evil had but one clear-cut cause, it would be more rational than it is.

As we examine the theosophical explanations, let us bear in mind that they must be received in the same way as all theosophical lore, in freedom and in full realization that all such statements can only be fingers pointing at the moon or like stages in *jnana yoga*, exercises to be worked through on the road to deeper and deeper realization. Some may be more important than others. Some may be allegories or even among the "blinds" of which H. P. Blavatsky spoke. Yet all these perspectives are, I think, worth studying insofar as they reflect the complexity of the "problem of evil" (or the problem of suffering, as it would more likely be called in the East).

For though the theosophical explanations are several, it is worth noting what they leave out. None display the defiant personal antagonist in rebellion against the personal patriarchal Father-God of Western monotheism, nor do any suggest a riotous polytheism in which careless or malicious spirits may do wickedness out of sheer caprice. Rather, all disharmonies can be understood as conditions logically inherent in a manifested consciousness-matter universe, or inseparable from the struggles and dangers embedded in the developmental path sentient beings in such a universe must follow. Let us now look at these explanations one after the other.

1. THE BINARY NATURE OF REALITY

H.P. Blavatsky in several places in *The Secret Doctrine* suggests that when the One became two, and then further subdivision takes place, evil is let in. She points out that the Pythagoreans "hated the Binary," believing that the "*One* was alone good"; for with the coming of two or more, the road forks and diverges into Good and Evil (IV, 146/II:574-575).

As the light of expressed creation spreads out it may be called God or Satan. *Demon est deus inversus.* In the complexity of the forking road life and death, good and evil both present themselves, "for death on earth becomes life on another plane" (IV:82/II:513).

We read also that duality is "the origin of Evil, or Matter"—referring back to the breakdown of the original outflow into subject and object, spirit and matter, of which we have already spoken. This does not mean that matter as such is evil, but rather that the dualism, and then the manyness, ingrained in the coexistence of matter and spirit is the inevitable seedbed of discord and thus of evil. For when many different entities—atoms, molecules, and the rest— are put into play, any number of possible combinations will emerge, not all benign one to another.

For that matter, this does not mean that the material universe of multiplicity is real in every sense of the word. Misperceptions on this score are part of the problem. Physical nature is "a bundle of most varied illusions on the plane of deceptive perceptions" in which "every pain and suffering [is] but the necessary pangs of incessant procreation" (*The Secret Doctrine* IV:43/II:475). Even more fundamental than the multiplicity of the material side of creation as a cause of evil is the difficult relationship between it and the spirit side. For spirit tends to see the material universe as other than itself and capable of imposing harsh limitations on it—making us think we are, say, a soul trapped in a fleshly casket—rather than understanding that matter is to be a co-operator with spirit's evolution.

The real solution to the problem of evil, we are here told in *The Secret Doctrine*, lies in understanding the truth about human nature. It is more than the transitory physical, it is "the divine within the animal" (IV:44/II:476). Human nature has a destiny that is only tangential to external nature, though at present painfully intertwined with it.

A first clue regarding evil, then, is that its "blockage" quality may not be what it seems. We see only the outer half of what is going on; what appears to be death may really be greater life.

2. EVOLUTION

The reason for apparent duality is the way in which the universe and all the teeming beings who dwell in it are evolving. When the One first extended itself into creation, there was, as we have seen, a kind of "fall"—a necessary involvement with the limitation and dualism inherent in changing forms. What comes into being cannot abide but must change and so "die" to one form, as it passes through the Cycle of Necessity on the great pilgrimage back to the One.

"God is light and Satan is the necessary Darkness or *Shadow* to set it off, without which pure Light would be invisible and incomprehensible" (*The Secret Doctrine*. IV:79/II:510). This force or light serves "to create and destroy" insofar as it is the "finite in the Infinite." The Satan principle involves death and rebirth in new forms as its necessary work moves forward. It is like a reducing valve which, as entities make their pilgrimage through the seven globes and various Races, gradually forces light into matter more and more. This permits the Pilgrims to experience matter in all its riotous multiplicity before it is slowly released again for the return.

The nature of evolution is to change, and therefore it destroys, even though its course is upward as it returns after involution to its eternal source. One cause of apparent evil, then, is the process of evolution. The blockage of one creature or species may be only for the sake of allowing a more advanced form to take its place as evolution moves forward.

To say that, however, is to deal only superficially with the real, and often uncomprehended, pain of the frightened individual creature. Theosophy has little sympathy for materialistic Darwinism and its casual acceptance of "Nature red in tooth and claw." Rather, it seeks to show, through the concept of karma, that the suffering of individuals is ultimately evolutionary in intent.

3. KARMA

Karma, the "Absolute and Eternal Law in the World of Manifestation" (*The Secret Doctrine* II:306/II:510) is the impersonal force which brings retribution dictated by each being through thoughts, words, and deeds—not by "destroying intellectual and individual liberty" (ibid.) but in order to demonstrate that we must live with the consequences of our choices.

Karma can, of course, also be beneficent; good deeds and thoughts produce favorable results. Nevertheless, along with happiness and opportunity, all human suffering, in fact, is finally attributable to karma and so to human free will, whatsoever attendant cause may also be involved.

Yet karma is not a "blockage" any more than is evolution, for though it may seem to obstruct the development of a life when it brings sickness, disaster, or premature death, yet it does not hinder but rather advances evolution through the free flow of spiritual cause. "Intimately, or rather indissolubly, connected with karma, then, is the Law of Rebirth, or of the reincarnation of the same spiritual individuality in a long, almost interminable, series of Personalities... like the various characters played by the same actor" (*The Secret Doctrine* III:307/II:306). Again, the apparent evil caused by karmic retribution is ultimately an illusion of partial vision which sees the outer result but not the inner cause and consequence.

We may, of course, ask why it has to be this way in the first place. Could there not have been a universe without karma because it was perfect from the beginning and never lost that perfection, hence had no need for salutary retribution? This query can have several possible answers.

a. First, those who want to live in such a perfect universe can. That is the condition attributed in effect to God-realized beings in all spiritual traditions, to saints and buddhas and sages. Their wisdom and compassion transcends all that can hurt or hinder. Though surrounded by the karmic universe, they are untouched by it, and for them it does not exist save as the realm where their compassion must operate. Karma exists only for those who act as though it does.

b. Second, as we have seen, the universe of matter and multiplicity exists as a force-field in which interaction—call it karma—takes place between entities on some level. To call for the abolishment of karma in a universe of matter and multiplicity is to call for a contradiction in terms. It would be simply to ask the abolishment of the universe as such and for the reunion of all things in the inchoate nameless Root.

c. Thus, the karmic field simply *is*. To ask why is as far beyond the reach of human mind as to ask why there is being itself. In theosophy, karma—and so its fruits—is not to be laid at the feet of a jealous god but is just the way things are and must be if there is being at all. The good news is that the shadow side of karma is as insubstantial compared to the splendid hope ahead of us as are the shades of night compared to sunrise.

d. A clue to karma's necessity lies in the theosophical identity of consciousness and the ultimate nature of reality. For thought is a constant process of shifting change, moving from cause to effect, finally unifying entities in a single integrating thought as will seeking joy moves to its consummation. If the universe is a great thought, it must separate, test relationships and interactions, and then unite.

4. Initiation

Yet another intepretation of evil, in the sense of suffering, is related to theosophy's widespread use of the language of initiation into the Mysteries. Initiation means accelerated growth in wisdom and a rapid expansion of awareness of the inner realities of things. This cannot be brought about without the transformation of the self—a process which, whether carried out in ritual or in the midst of the experiences of life, is like speeded-up evolution. There is that which must be destroyed and that which must be quickened. Thus H.P. Blavatsky describes the

"Twelve Tortures" of the ancient Egyptian initiation (*The Secret Doctrine*, V:290; *The Esoteric Writings of H.P. Blavatsky*, p. 241). C.W. Leadbeater tells us that the fourth initiation on the path of adepthood parallels the crucifixion of Christ, and so includes suffering, the greatest of which is not physical but the aloneness that is the dark night of the soul.

The suffering of initiation may be sought deliberately, or one may, so to speak, be pulled through it. It may be "programmed" as a mystery rite, like the often hard and painful initiations of Native American cultures. Or, it may be one of life's "natural" initiations, from birth through maturation to sickness and death. In any case though the anguish is real, it can be borne without complaint by the candidate who knows its meaning and can envision the goal.

5. BLACK MAGIC

A major theme of Blavatsky's first book, *Isis Unveiled*, is that magic demonstrates the existence of nonmaterial reality and so is an invaluable indicator of the true inner nature of things. Yet, if white magic exists, so also must black magic. We are told several times of its possibility and reality (e.g. *The Secret Doctrine* V:37-38/*Esoteric Writings*, pp. 37-38), although Blavatsky does not take all accounts of black magic at face value.

First, a word to the reader. The notion of black magic is likely to give rise to wild and bizarre images or suggest something better left to fantasy fiction or sensational tabloids. We must realize, though, that for theosophy magic really refers simply to power exercised through consciousness. We all practice magic all the time when through our conscious will we control ourselves or influence others. Magic is "black" if that power is exerted for self-centered ends. On this level, then, magic is no more and no less mysterious than ordinary consciousness inter-acting with body and environment. Insofar as such faculties as clairvoyance, telepathy, or psychokinesis are real, their role in the implementation of such magic, white or black, cannot be discounted. But however and by whomever exercised, whether called black magic or not, the real exercise of evil on the hu-man plane is always linked to human selfishness, cal-lousness, and cruelty, not to "occult forces" in them-selves. These latter are as neutral as the knife held in the human hand and controlled by the human mind, which may be used to chop vegetables or to kill.

The Mahatma Letters refers from time to time to *dugpas*, Tibetan black magicians who can cause a great deal of localized evil. They are said to provoke vanity (p. 365) and are even given permission to de-ceive chelas, disciples of Masters, for the student's own ultimate good (p. 229). They sowed dissension in the London Lodge (p. 477), for those who are "most devoted to the Cause, Masters, Theosophy, call it by whatever name—*are those that are the most tried*" (ibid.).

More powerful than the *dugpas* are the Dark Chohans (Ma-Mo Chohans)—imperfect "gods," or rather black magicians on a cosmic scale, who play a dominant role in the cycles of dissolution of ages and worlds and spread ignorance and destruction (pp. 455-56). But the Masters of the Light have no right to impede such work nor that of the dugpas, for it has its purpose, so long as its agents obey occult laws and do not cross the paths of their betters.

We see therefore that certain specific examples of evil, perhaps even on a planetary scale, may not be the result of evolution or karma directly. Rather it may result from a particular individualized consciousness who has mastered certain occult arts and employs them—as is his prerogative under the laws of karma and free will—for evil ends which may work harm to others.

But though he meant it for ill, higher powers than the black adept's can turn it to good, and the evil may ultimately redound to spiritual growth for someone or some world. It may be that certain particularized outbreaks of evil in human history, especially those that are utterly nonrational and disproportionate to the events that caused them—famine, pointless violence and war, cruelty and persecutions, whether those of Nazi Germany or more recently in Cambodia—are the work of some powerful dark magus of this sort whose hand reached for a brief span into human history. This interpretation would in no way relieve the responsibility of those who, by active or passive choice, allowed themselves to become the human vehicles of that dark enchantment. But it can permit speculation on the "deep background" of episodes which otherwise seem out of place, even in the oft-gloomy annals of human history.

6. Religion

In a celebrated passage, *The Mahatma Letters* tell us that "evil is the exaggeration of good, the progeny of human selfishness and greediness" and that "save death—which is no evil but a necessary law, and accidents which will always find their reward in a future life—the *origin* of every evil whether small or great is in human action, in man whose intelligence makes him the one free agent in Nature."

We are here told it is excess above the normal needs of life—selfishness in food and drink, sex and shelter, travel and pleasure—that produces one-third of human evil. For the rest: "I will point out the greatest, the chief cause of nearly two-thirds of the evils that pursue humanity ever since that cause became a power. It is religion under whatever form and in whatsoever nation." (p. 57)

This statement sounds surprising—even shocking—at first glance, yet a moment's reflection will reveal its truth. It is not intended as an attack on religion as such. Rather, it is a blunt observation of how religion, broadly defined, is far too often used in human life.

Simple animal selfishness and hedonism do not account for the greatest and most pervasive evils in human history. The foulest massacres, the most degrading exploitation, the wickedest perversions of truth and beauty have not been committed merely to pander to ordinary greed but for the sake of something supposedly higher, often by zealots who for the sake of their cause have themselves sacrificed much. This "something higher" takes many forms—God or the gods, faith, pride of tribe or class or country, the revolutionary impulse which seeks to destroy all, that (as it believes) all may be reborn fresh and pure.

In the past, these causes were usually identified with religion in the conventional sense, with the will of God or the battle-frenzy of a tribal Wotan. In more recent times the names of the gods have changed to such abstractions as nation, race, and ideology. But they all come under the definition suggested by the cited passage from The Mahatma Letters, which goes on in the next sentence to say, "It is the sacerdotal caste, the priesthood and the churches; it is in those illusions that man looks upon as sacred, that he has to search out the source of that multitude of evils which is the great curse of humanity and that almost overwhelms mankind" (pp. 57-58). On the basis of twentieth-century experience, surely it is no great extrapolation to include among "those illusions that man looks upon as sacred" the blinding passions of distorted nationalism and ideology, and in the "sacerdotal caste" the propagandists and secular messiahs who have fed these and fed upon them.

In our own century, the evil wrought by simple greed, great as it is, pales beside that brought about by such faiths as imperialism, Nazism, Communism, nationalism, and resurgent fundamentalism within a number of religions. These enslavements of the spirit, possibly abetted by black magic, clearly count for more than mere thralldom to the flesh.

Yet we must remember again that "evil is the exaggeration of good." Religion, however broadly defined, is certainly not evil per se. Indeed, it may be a matter of the worst being a corruption of the best. Religion, insofar as it represents a yearning after something more than mere material existence, an effort of the divine within to break free and be itself, an assertion that the ultimate causes and ends are spiritual, is the impulse to truth. But how easily this aspiration becomes satisfied with partial truths which become idols clung to with all the passion proper to the whole truth and becomes diverted into the evil of which religion is capable!

The theosophical attitude toward religion can easily be oversimplified and misunderstood. Blavatsky and other classic theosophical writers vehemently attacked whole colleges of theologians. Yet they also affirmed that a core of truth lies in all religions and that, at the inception of each, lies the work of a Master of the Wisdom who enshrined in its central symbols important elements of the ancient truth than which no religion is higher. Not all religion is equally good or bad, and in all there is at least a potential for good as well as for evil. We shall examine this question in more detail in the next chapter.

7. JEHOVAH-SATAN

The Secret Doctrine devotes much attention to a complex argument that Jehovah and Satan are one and the same. In this context Jehovah is to be distinguished from God as the Infinite Reality behind the outflowings of creation and Satan from the serpent of Eden, who is the "Bright Angel" Lucifer, the "Light Bearer" who conveys only wise advice.

This argument may seem puzzling and disturbing to many readers and out of keeping with the tone they perceive in theosophical literature elsewhere. To what degree it may be taken as allegory or symbol is open. The case may be brought entirely, if one wishes, under *The Secret Doctrine*'s declaration elsewhere:

> To some extent, it is admitted that even the Esoteric Teaching is allegorical. To make the latter comprehensible to the average intelligence, the use of symbols cast in an intelligible form is needed. Hence the allegorical and semi-mythical narratives in the exoteric, and the only *semi*-metaphysical and objective representations in the Esoteric Teachings. For the purely and transcendentally spiritual conceptions are adapted only to the perceptions of those who *"see without eyes, hear without ears, and sense without organs."* (III:90-91/II:81)

However, some treatment here of the Jehovah/Satan material is called for, because it comes up sometimes in discussion of theosophical literature, including that of its adversaries, and because it appeals to a deep sense many have of the "fallen" nature of our world as it is. I would also like to stress that the use of Hebrew terminology in such discussions simply derives from ancient Gnostic usage and has nothing to do with a critique of Judaism as a religion. With this Blavatsky was on excellent terms, as is shown by her extensive employment of the Kabbala, the Jewish mystical system. Indeed, Kabbalism has its ultimate roots in the same thought-world as Gnosticism; both are related attempts to find deep levels of inner meaning within the Hebrew scriptures.

In these *Secret Doctrine* passages, as in certain ancient Gnostic systems, the Jehovah-Satan figure represents a lower creator whose division of humanity into male and female was the real cause of trouble in the Garden of Eden, not the serpent's sage advice to eat of the tree of the knowledge of good and evil. "The appelation Sa'tan, in Hebrew Sātān . . . belongs by right to the first and cruellest 'Adversary' *of all the other Gods*—Jehovah" (III:386/II:387). "Satan represents metaphysically simply the *reverse* or the *polar opposite* of everything in Nature. He is the 'Adversary', allegorically, the 'Murderer', and the great Enemy of *all*, because there is nothing in the whole Universe that has not two sides—the reverses of the same medal. But in that case, light, goodness, beauty, etc., may be called Satan with as much propriety as the Devil, since they are the Adversaries of darkness, badness and ugliness." (III:388/II:389)

Thus the idea of Satan can be taken to represent merely the necessary dualism of manifested existence, to which we have referred above under 1. Nevertheless, as the "lower creator" theme suggests, *The Secret Doctrine* also shows considerable sympathy for the position of those ancient Gnostic groups which saw Jehovah-Satan as "a proud, ambitious, and impure Spirit who has abused his power by usurping the place of the *Highest God*, though he was no better, and in some respects far worse than his *brother Elohim*; the latter representing the all-embracing, manifested Deity . . . " (ibid.).

Here, and in *Isis Unveiled* (II:184), Blavatsky commends the myth of those Gnostics who said that Jehovah-Satan, often named Ilda-Baoth, was a proud spirit who set out to create a world of his own but bungled the job and left only a flawed earth peopled by monstrous creatures. Yet he could not prevent man from possessing a soul which linked him to his wise mother, Sophia (Wisdom), and the light of the supreme Being. As man aspired toward higher things, Ilda-Baoth was filled with rage toward his own creation and sought—as he still does—to destroy his handiwork. Bearing in mind that this Gnostic allegory informs us that Ilda-Baoth was aided in his labor by his malicious sons, the planetary spirits, we find the matter well summed up in a striking passage in *The Secret Doctrine:*

> The One is infinite and unconditioned. It cannot create, for It can have no relation to the finite and conditioned. If everything we see, from the glorious suns and planets down to the blades of grass and the specks of dust, had been created by the Absolute Perfection and were the direct work of even the *First* Energy that proceeds from It, then every such thing would have been perfect, and unconditioned, like its author. The millions upon millions of imperfect works found in Nature testify loudly that they are the products of finite, conditioned beings—though the latter were and are Dhyan Chohans, Archangels, or whatever else they may be named. In short, these imperfect

works are the unfinished production of evolution, under the guidance of imperfect Gods. (V:213-14/*The Esoteric Writings of H.P. Blavatsky*, p. 181)

We see here a subtheme of *The Secret Doctrine* and other theosophical sources which is, among other things, yet another interpretation of evil, that the actual creation as we know it is the handiwork of chains of relatively imperfect "gods" ranging between our level and the Ultimate. In particular, it is to be laid at the doorstep of an arrogant but incompetent blunderer like Ilda-Baoth.

Whether one thinks of such propositions as literally or only allegorically true, they can meet an "existential" need for dealing with evil which goes beyond just attributing it to various "laws." Such explanations do not entirely satisfy the rage and despair the world's suffering evokes. We still want to ask over and over, why does a universe which contains even "rational" evil have to exist at all? Even if evil can be explained as necessitated by karma, by the evolutionary process, by the fundamental dualism which manifestation entails, the question still remains as to the necessity for so much suffering.

One answer is that the God of this world is, at best, imperfect and, at worst, a vindictive, incompetent blunderer into whose world we, whose true home is in halls of light far above his sway, are entrapped until, by following the slow path of evolution and initiation, we free ourselves from his grasp.

Perhaps we do need to follow the Cycle of Necessity: We need to move through the chains of worlds and races. It is necessary that we experience choice and the realm of matter, because a dualism of spirit and matter is "built-in" to a universe of manifestation and separateness, and choice is incumbent in a universe whose reality is also the unity of consciousness and matter. Still we might feel that there is more behind the extent of evil we know in this world. Something went wrong. A malevolent though finite entity pretending to be a god is also loose in our particular corner of the space-time continuum, where he has fouled the relationship of spirit and matter, leaving us more deeply trapped in space and time than need be. The notion that this world with its laws was made by imperfect beings, without the direct license of the supreme One whose nature we share but who does not directly create, can be a supportive idea.

Those higher yet impure beings should not, however, be made scapegoats and excuses for human folly. If lords of darkness, whether *dugpas* or maddened gods, spoil our world, it is because, in some way, we have let them do so.

SUMMING UP

Let us reflect on the truth that ours is an appropriate —even propitious—time to discuss the problem of evil. Not only have the manifold horrors of our age brought home to us the urgency of the problem, but they have shattered many illusions and many complacent misunderstandings of the scope and depth and tenaciousness of evil. Such awareness should be no stranger to theosophists, who see the history of our globe scarred with many catclysms unexpected by most, and marked by the rise and fall of race upon race, nation upon nation, empire upon proud empire.

In the high noon of Europe's nineteenth-century confidence and global domination, for example, Helena Blavatsky proved a better prophet (or rather recorder of prophecy) than many when she wrote, "It is simply knowledge, and mathematically correct computations, which enable the WISE MEN OF THE EAST to foretell, for instance, that England is on the eve of such or another catastrophe; that France is nearing such a point of her Cycle; and that Europe in general is threatened with, or rather is on the eve of, a cataclysm to which her own Cycle of racial *Karma has led her*" (*The Secret Doctrine* II:371/I:646). These and similar lines were discussed in an interesting article, "H.P.B. and the War," which appeared in *The Theosophist* (Adyar) of August, 1940, just after the fall of France to Hitler's armies, when all appeared dark indeed to those the magazine elsewhere spoke of as the Forces of Good, and of Light.

Ours is, in the words of Jacob Needleman, a "time between dreams." Old comfortable beliefs—in dogmatic religion, in progress, in human goodness—have been shattered, at least in the naive forms they were held only a few generations, or even a few decades, ago. One era is gone; the new dreams have not yet arisen.

Now, however, in a time of waking from dogmatic slumbers, before a possible next sleep, we can, if we have the courage, probe more deeply into the real condition of humanity and of nature than is possible when under the spell of pleasant fantasies. It is a dark time, but in darkness what light there is shines all the brighter. As we face evil unflinchingly we know its reality. If we do not succumb to the temptations of stylish melancholy or hopeless despair, but gaze clear-eyed upon evil's hideous face we can perceive its contours and features well. Knowing the shape of the dragon, we can ascertain where best to thrust the lance.

Theosophy offers weapons to fight evil and fend off despair. We can contain the power of evil by understanding its purpose in karma and evolution;

its initiatory role; its necessity to the universe of manifestation; its sometime origins in black magic which can be combatted; its roots in spiritual illusions and cosmic entities above which we can rise.

We can realize there is that in each of us which never has been, and can never be, wholly under the power of any evil. For its nature comes from realms higher than evil's reach, and to them it will return.

6
Veiled Truth

In II. P. Blavatsky's *Isis Unveiled*, we are told that "truth remains one, and there is not a religion, whether Christian or heathen, that is not firmly built upon the rock of ages—God and immortal spirit" (I:467). In the same source, there is also reference to "the remote past, during those ages when every true religion was based on knowledge of the occult powers of nature" (I:25).

As we have seen, ideas absolutely fundamental to theosophy include the primacy of consciousness as the creative principle in both the cosmos and the individual human being, the brotherhood of humanity, and the existence of hidden "powers latent in man" which, utilizing the subtle matter/energy of the inner planes, can affect outward manifestations. In *Isis Unveiled* we see that, according to the preeminent modern theosophical teacher, it is precisely upon these same concepts that all religion is based. For "God and immortal spirit" are none other than consciousness as the *a priori* in both the universe and the individual respectively. The fact that this truth is common to the religions of all humanity makes human brotherhood not only an ideal but on a deeper level also *a priori* truth. So likewise does a notion of a "remote past," when occult powers which ought to be the common heritage of all human beings were the basis of "every true religion."

This general perspective seems to be borne out by what can be gleaned of the spiritual life of our first human ancestors from archaeology—most of it discovered since the publication of *Isis Unveiled* in 1877. To be sure, our picture of the religion of the Paleolithic, or Old Stone Age, will never—at least by ordinary scientific means—be more than fragmentary. But fascinating hints exist.

Paleolithic culture was general until the discovery of agriculture in some parts of the earth around 12,000 years ago, when what is usually called the Neolithic, or New Stone Age, way of life was inaugurated. It persisted in other places into the twentieth century. The first creatures accounted human by scientific criteria appeared some six million years earlier, the first known stone tools about one million years ago, and the first possible evidences of religious attitudes, such as burial practices, about 100,000 years back. Lavish, if often enigmatic, evidence of spiritual perspectives, such as the famous cave paintings, commence around 30,000 B.C.E.

Over such vast stretches of time, there survive today only those tokens of spiritual life which were fabricated of bone or stone or were well protected in the deep interior of caves. The myths, the songs, the dances, the perhaps immense panoply of symbols and ritual implements made of more fragile materials—of wood, skins, or feathers—the artwork and altars exposed to the open air, all these are forever lost, and so is the interpretive context they would give to what we do have. Some help, of course, is offered by anthropological studies of contemporary societies which seem to be on a cultural level similar to the prehistoric people under consideration, but while such comparisons are often very suggestive, they can never be more than conjecture.

Nonetheless, I believe that we do have enough evidence of the religion of prehistoric Paleolithic man to show that it was in fact centered on God, immortal spirit, and the occult powers of nature. The mute records which have spanned the long millennia testify to these essential areas of awareness. They also hint at how religious life might have been experienced in earlier worlds and Races.

The earliest remains which, so far as we can tell, pertain to religion involve burial. Bones of the deceased from as early as 100,000 years ago show that care was taken to bury them, to orient them east and west, and to accompany them with stone tools and parts of animals. Whether this care was taken out of love or fear we cannot tell, but the essential point remains—precautions concerning the mortal remains of a person imply a belief that something immortal survives, to be helped or propitiated as it continues its pilgrimage through endless time. Somewhat later bones are painted ocher, suggesting the color of blood and therefore life, or buried in a foetal position, sending us a message across many thousands of years that for these early humans, death, despite appearances, did not have the final victory. Life hovered nearby and rebirth was to come.

The elaborate arrangements of the skulls of bears and other animals taken by those ancient hunters, found in caves or around dwellings, indicate the same idea. Like hunting peoples today, they lived spiritually very close to the animal kindreds upon which they depended and were well aware that within them too dwelt soul, soul which circulated from life to life and which retained power even after physical death.

The famous cave paintings of France and Spain give us the same message even more vividly. First, it must be realized that these remarkable works deep in the hidden places of the earth were no mere picture galleries, nor simply the ornamentation of homes. Containing almost invariably pictures of game animals, the painted walls and ceilings are far down in caves, much beyond living areas near the entrance and sometimes in caves which show no sign of ever having been inhabited. Then as now, the pictures can be reached only by an arduous passage through narrow corridors; in some cases the paintings can be seen only by assuming very awkward positions. Clearly, the artworks are the centerpieces of a sanctuary, a sacred space far from the surface or the places where people lived their daily lives. To reach them would have been a difficult pilgrimage, an ordeal or initiation. One can only imagine what those graceful beasts and bright colors could have meant to an early man who had come to them after a hard and dangerous journey through labyrinthean underground tunnels, guided only by a flickering torch, when its light suddenly fell upon them in a hidden place probably reserved for secret rites or magic and initiation.

The exact purpose of these animal forms, painted over and over, sometimes superimposed on each other, is unknown. No doubt one purpose had to do with hunting magic: occult lines of force connected these bright figures made by human hands in the sanctuaries with their counterparts in forest and field. Painting and ceremonially killing animals in the sanctuary might produce similar results in the chase. The caves may also have been places of initiation of children into adulthood within the tribe; this would be an appropriate place for new initiates to pass that time apart from ordinary life and close to the gods or spirits, which is characteristic of initiation, and to learn the lore of the tribe, which no doubt had much to do with the myth and magic of the animals here portrayed. In one cave footprints in a room just adjacent to the gallery indicate the dancing or stomping of a large number of childish feet, which could well be a souvenir of such an initiatory scenario from before the last Ice Age.

John E. Pfeiffer in *The Creative Explosion: An Inquiry into the Origins of Art and Religion* has suggested a further though related purpose of cave art: that the caves themselves, with their various passages, their natural and artificial landmarks, their several panels of art, were aids to memory and storehouses of tribal wisdom. After one has walked a number of times through a cave, he says, one begins to get a feeling that one is *meant* to experience it in a certain sequence and to see features in order, from now one angle and now another. In the whole is embedded a people's lore, to be transmitted from one generation to another, as though one were walking through a gigantic book. If its script could be resolved, we would find stories, places, rites, perhaps even theology and philosophy.

Obviously, an interpretation like this—which is supported by analogies with more recent rock painting in Africa and Australia—fits very well with the initiation theme. It is not inconsistent with hunting magic, though it informs us that sorcery far from exhausts the meaning of these underground temples.

Rather, we are told that, in a way which seems congruous with the spirit of theosophical wisdom (though this is not the purport of Pfeiffer's inquiry), deep in the past man was aware, if only half-consciously, of profound truths which he could express only in symbols and by staging initiatory, mind- and soul-opening scenarios.

For certain, the cave as lore-book and temple indicates occult relationships. It bespeaks correspondences between inner and outer, between the heart of the earth and what transpires on its surface, between the animal and its below-ground magical model. At the same time the cave tells us, like the burial practices, of immortal spirit. It implies that animals—and by extension humans—have a life which is more than the material frame.

As for God or universal spirit, that is less easy to read in the "hard" remains of paleolithic culture, for it could well be an idea beyond symbolic expression, communicated only in the song and story of the ritual, or even only in its silences. Not a few peoples today on a very simple level of material culture have a notion of a High God or Great Spirit, well above the various nature and ancestral spirits who are also part of the pantheon, a God who created the world and established its moral order, yet who is seldom portrayed and perhaps only invoked in dire emergency. Yet, if it is true that the caves represent elaborate, generation-spanning repositories of lore, it would seem that some sense of transcendent spiritual unity and meaning must undergird them. Like theosophy, or any other coherent philosophy, they would suggest the unity of knowledge. They would imply the reality of a Great Plan in which the turning of the seasons and the lives of all that breathe are interwoven. That in turn would point to universal as well as individual consciousness. Later, the great megalithic monuments like Stonehenge, which seem to have been at once astronomical observatories and portals of the Other World, at once a temple and a scientific laboratory, present still more forcefully the interlinking of spirit and cosmos.

Perhaps the most spectacular of all features of primal religion is shamanism. The shaman is suggested by one or two cave-painting figures, notably the famous "Great Sorcerer" of the Trois-Frères Cave, France, which appears to be a human form dressed in animal skins and horned. But it is in recent anthropological accounts, above all from Siberians, Eskimos, and Native Americans, that shamanism truly comes to life. The "classic" shaman, as described by Mircea Eliade in *Shamanism: Archaic Techniques of Ecstasy,* is an individual who initially receives a call from the gods in the form of voices and seizures; he must get them under control or be driven mad. He handles this "initiatory psychopathology" through an ordeal in the wild, under the supervision of a senior shaman, or even in sickness and feverish dreams, which is like a death and rebirth. If he is successful, his voices become subject to spirits able to help him. He can now go into trance in which he flies to the far corners of the earth, visits the worlds of the gods and departed spirits, and heals by seeking out wandering souls or defeating evil spirits of sickness or madness. In many cultures the shaman was an important person whose performances were major events, and who combined the functions of loremaster, physician, and psychiatrist.

Indeed, there are those who suggest that the experience of shamanism was the ultimate origin of human religion. The adept's encounter with invisible entities, and his supernatural powers, suggested

God, immortal spirit, and occult powers to early man. These constitute the foundations of a world-view that embraced more than the material and was perpetuated not only in the shaman's enactments but also in myth and ritual. The power of the shamanic vision can be seen in the account of the Eskimo shaman's initiation by the Danish explorer Rasmussen. He speaks of the *angakok*, or tutelary spirit, which the candidate shaman receives as a "mysterious light" he suddenly senses within his frame. This enables him to see not only far away but into past and future and spiritual realms, so that he can "discover souls, stolen souls, which are either kept concealed in far, strange lands, or have been taken up or down to the Land of the Dead." For such a one, clearly the spiritual world, initiation, and the occult powers wielded by the wise are very real.

In the Neolithic era, the New Stone Age of archaic agriculture, the spiritual focus shifts to Mother Earth. Farming brought much that was good: stability in one place, a relatively more dependable food supply, villages and towns and eventually cities, a rapidly expanding human population leading to division of labor. Yet in the mythological accounts of the discovery of agriculture, we sometimes find it portrayed as a sort of fall, marked by a crime: the killing of a beautiful maiden out of whose body came the various crops, or a heartless cutting into the flesh of Mother Earth.

Religiously, too, the Neolithic era shows an upsurge in the dark magical side of belief in spirit, referred to in theosophical accounts of a debased Atlantis. It is here, not in the Old Stone Age, that headhunting, and animal and human sacrifice, proliferate. For with agriculture comes fresh awareness that life and death are intertwined and that fertility requires victims. The seed must die and be buried before it sprouts; the shrunken head of an enemy danced through the fields will give them its still-potent life force. For life to continue generation after generation, the first-fruits, including one's first-born, should be sacrificed to the gods who hold all weather and the fruit of all wombs in their hands. In this stage too we find much increased sexual antagonism, an undercurrent of tension between men and women, marked by separate secret societies for each sex, often with horrendous initiatory ordeals. Perhaps the antagonism paralleled the new sacred power given women by agriculture with its fresh emphasis on fecundity and the mother goddess.

In any event, the Neolithic revolution was accompanied by dark magic of a sort not unfamiliar to theosophical lore. In its ambiguous aura began the human population explosion, the ancient slave empires, and the burgeoning technology which set humanity on its headlong rush through those last few millennia of history that have brought us to where we are today.

Religious Decline and Renewal

We are then brought to an equally important theosophical concept concerning religion, its decline. Religions, we are told in *Isis Unveiled*, "in time become adulterated" (II:536). This is partly due to priestly corruption and partly to the differing cultural settings and historical vicissitudes of every faith. Religion which had as its original impulses awareness of God and immortal spirit, and wisdom concerning the occult powers of nature, slides in the direction of those illusions which *The Mahatma Letters* had informed us were the origin of two-thirds of the world's evil. Knowledge of the mighty secrets beneath the world of appearances is a tremendous lever for good or ill, whether on the part of the shaman/wizard in his dark wood at the dawn of human life in this world, or that of the modern nuclear physicist.

The decline of religion, I would say, should not be thought of as a "straight-line" phenomenon. Opportunities for the misuse of any religion abound at both its beginning and its end, and the historical trajectory of all religions has brought alike temptations and opportunities for enhanced understanding all along its course. To take the example of Christianity, in the twentieth century it has produced saints who have manifested its spiritual power as well as could be hoped for, while if the letters of the Apostle Paul and the Book of Acts are any guide, corruption was not wanting in the first century. Yet it is true that as religions with their priesthoods and institutions grow and prosper, so will their corruptibility. As the world turns and a religion's original message seems couched in less and less current language, the temptation will grow to sustain its life by the sort of identifications of the faith with ethnicity, nationalism, respectability, or sheer magical power that quickly lead to evil. So it was, perhaps, with the old Paleolithic nature- and soul-wisdom in the new world of life and death on the farm.

The Neolithic world became the world of the Bronze Age, the Iron Age, and the age of the ancient agricultural empires in the Near East, India, and China. In this age came a remarkable turning-point in human spiritual life. The ancient world saw the appearance of a set of great religious figures who lent their authority, and often their names, to a new form of religious life, the great historical religions. They include the Buddha and Buddhism, Confucius and Confucianism, Lao-tzu and Taoism, and the more mythical Krishna of Hinduism in its later forms. Subsequently came Jesus and Christianity, and Muhammad and Islam.

These faiths, which now dominate the religious world, are significantly different from the religion of the Old and New Stone Ages, for they can be traced (except Hinduism) to a single founder and single moment in historical time. Needless to say, in actual fact they all owe much to influences other than the teaching of that one person, and all experienced much historical development over the centuries. Yet their heart would be missing without that person, place, and time—and the theme of a special revelation at a special point within historical time, so different from the "cosmic religion" centered on the cycles of animal life or of seed time and harvest that went before. For special revelation focused on a special person, place, and time, recorded in a special scripture, is crucial to the self-understanding of this new generation of religions.

The pivot of this great change was the fifth century B.C.E., approximately the time of the Buddha, Confucius, Lao-tzu, and Zoroaster. In Hinduism it was the time the old Vedic religion was beginning to give way to the mystical wisdom of the Upanishads and the outlook symbolized, at least, by the Krishna of the *Bhagavad-Gita*. Further west, it was roughly the time of the great Hebrew prophets and the earlier Greek philosophers. All across the globe momentous stirrings were underway as one spiritual age was yielding to another. The philosopher Karl Jaspers called it the Axial Age; its later fruit include Jesus and Muhammad and their religions, but in a real sense the latter was probably the "seal of the prophets" as claimed by Islam, for one does not envision new world-scale religions starting today in quite the same way as in the days of Jesus or Muhammad. Theirs was a unique work belonging to a unique era in human life.

Three of these religions—Buddhism, Christianity, and Islam—are truly international, having spread and planted themselves in a number of major culture-areas. Others, such as Hinduism, Confucianism, Taoism, and in a special sense Judaism, are essentially specific to one major culture.

They all share certain salient features intimately linked to the unique era in which they arose. First, the invention of writing had made possible the keeping of records of such lives as those of the founders. The writing of scripture was now possible, and scriptures were a new and immensely important feature of these religions in comparison to those of the Stone Ages. Second, the emergence of large empires or trading areas made relatively easy the dissemination of new faiths, and created political entities which cried out for ideologies more articulate than the old sacred kingships to hold them together. Third, the increasing complexity of societies, with their greater and greater division of labor and the relative rapidity with which new ways replaced old, increased the importance of the individual over against the old tribal unit. In some ways the splendor of the individual was enhanced, with his capacity for salvation or power; in others only his anxiety was increased before a cruel and baffling world. Either way, the time had come for the central symbol of a religion to be a person, a Buddha or Christ, living, transfigured, dying in the midst of known historical time, rather than the sacred mountain or the dying animal of yore.

Most significantly of all, the Axial Age was an age of the discovery of history. This came about only half-consciously, only gradually, and not by everyone—but slowly it became apparent that something was wrong, or at least incomplete, about the old cosmic religious notion of time moving in circles with each turning year. The new pace of change, the rise of empires and the march of technology, the evidence from records kept on parchment or clay, made evident that time also goes in an irreversible line, at least on the ordinary human level—that things change and do not change back.

With this realization came what Mircea Eliade has called the "terror of history"—dread of a world in which new things are always about to happen and nothing will stay put. To be sure, most unexpected things that happened to ordinary ancient people were likely to be bad—plague, famine, locusts, war and invading plunderers. So quickly, in fact, did the terror of history arise with history's discovery that the awareness that anything can happen in time was suppressed virtually before it could come to consciousness. But its ghost lingers in the many beliefs by which the Axial Age religions sought to counter it: 1) History is linear, but it is under God's control and will end with his judgment and incoming paradise. 2) One soon enough leaves this vale of tears to enjoy eternity in heaven. 3) One can transcend time in mystical experience, in an enlightenment like that of the Buddha. 4) What seems to be linear historical time is only a segment of a set of immense cycles, like the kalpas of Hinduism. 5) Ritual, like that so beloved of Confucianism, can create sacred, eternal times that reach outside time in some way and connect with that which is timeless.

Many of these attitudes, of course, are shared by

theosophy, for it does not absolutize historical time, though it does evaluate time positively as an arena of overall progress through Root Races. At the same time, the discovery-of-history era can be viewed in theosophical terms as the Fifth Race coming to full flower. Some of its leading teachers, such as the Buddha, Krishna, and Jesus, are considered fundamental Masters of the Fifth Race; each Race has its Manu and its Buddha, as well as other Masters particularly associated with it and its needs. The social complexification and growing technology which induced the consciousness of history, as well as the kind of analytic thought that they all reflect, are characteristic of the Fifth Race and part of its role in the course of human events. The Fifth Race Masters both augment the best of those discoveries, and also uphold and conserve the place of another side of human nature— that which transcends history—to a people whose very genius is likely to get them deeply enmeshed in temporality. It is no happenstance, then, that some of the greatest of the Masters were historical teachers of this era, or that their messages, diverse as they were, dealt with the problems of living in, yet transcending, the world of historical time. Their religions also became subject to the corruptions of which we have spoken, but have played an indispensible role in the evolution of the planet and the numerous Pilgrims enjoying its bounty and facing its terrors.

THEOSOPHY AND WORLD RELIGIONS

The theosophical view of the world's religions can, I think, be fairly summarized as follows. Behind the impulse which creates all genuine human religion lies a sense that human reality is not exhausted by our material nature. Or, to put it positively, behind religion lies awareness of "God and immortal spirit," however one may understand those terms.

To say that religion was also originally based on "knowledge of the occult powers of nature" is really to say nothing different, for the occult (i.e., hidden) truth of nature is that its visible, material form is but the expression of invisible, immaterial spiritual realities. These facts were better comprehended, at least intuitively, in the simpler human cultures of remote antiquity than now. Furthermore, the folk of those cultures were able to wield effectively the powers such comprehension gave, whether in the magical flight of the shaman or the power behind the glowing forms made by the cave-artist's brush. But with the ability to use such powers for good goes the opportunity to use them for evil.

Partly to counteract such evil, partly to teach humanity new lessons required by new occasions, have come wise teachers. They have been with humanity since its physical beginning, starting with the beings who took human form as teachers after their arrival in the midst of the Lemurian era. Such teachers have seen to it that not only have we been kept aware of "God and immortal spirit," but also have had veiled reminders of some important features of the ancient and eternal wisdom now known as theosophy. As H.P. Blavatsky demonstrated with some amplitude, certain symbols which the wise will associate with that wisdom occur over and over in the world's religions. Emblems based on the numbers three and seven, for example, are among them, to remind those who know of the divine Trinity in God and man, and of the theosophic "Law of Seven" which underlies the seven globes, seven planes, and seven Root Races—and subtly to prepare those who do not yet know for the reception of fuller wisdom at the right time.

A special "generation" of such teachers accompanies the ascent of a Root Race, when they become the founders of its religions and great civilizations. So it was with the Fifth Root Race, when it came into its own around the time of the Axial Age some twenty-five centuries ago. The great traditional religions and civilizations of its world, from Europe to China and later in the Americas, rather suddenly (in evolutionary terms) appeared on the stage of the world proclaiming such men as Confucius or Muhammad their geniuses.

These wise teachers are men who in some way had undergone initiatory experiences that gave them particular insight into spiritual reality. To put it another way, they were like humanizations of basic principles of that reality (for you *are* what you have experienced and know absolutely); Confucius was called coeval with Heaven and Earth, Jesus the Logos or Incarnate Word of God. They came to instruct and initiate humankind into a like oneness with Ultimate Reality, in ways suitable to various times and places.

Out of these teachings stem the great religions, and some lesser ones as well. All have doctrines and practices deriving from genuine awareness of the nonmaterial nature of ultimate reality and the possibility of initiation into deeper and deeper levels of awareness. But the shape of those doctrines and practices are modified, and not infrequently garbled, by cultural diversity over long stretches of historical time, and by the human proclivity to twist whatever we can lay our hands on to the service of egocentric power.

This picture is not incompatible with that offered by anthropology and the history of religions. Prehistoric religion, broadly speaking, was more similar around the globe than human religion has been since the Axial Age teachers brought the "great religions" into existence in historical time.

The religion of prehistoric men was united by awareness of the sacred, or nonmaterial reality, expressed through animistic belief in spirits, human and divine, by practices to experience that reality of the shamanistic sort, and by "cosmic religion" symbol systems which integrated human life into the turning of the seasons and to territorial space. Even in the "archaic" religion of Neolithic farmers and the ancient civilizations, more similarity probably obtained than subsequently. The names of gods and the details of rites varied immensely, yet the basic pattern of the religious life of, say, Japan before Buddhism, Egypt prior to Christ or Muhammad, and pre-Christian Britain was perhaps more comparable than today. Three thousand years ago, when the Buddha, Christ, and the Prophet were as yet unborn, all enjoyed some version of archaic cosmic religion. Wizards and shamans were in the land, monuments like Stonehenge, the Great Pyramid, and the holy mountains of Japan showed the importance everywhere of orientation to sky and sacred space, and worship consisted basically of offering food to deities at their altar-homes.

The great religions arose over a period of a millennium or more in complex interaction with the invention of writing, the discovery of history, and the emergence of large political systems. Thus they are characterized by scriptures, a need to deal with "the terror of history," and the need to unify human spiritual experience even as the archaic empires sought to unify secular life. They tended toward establishing normative doctrines, laws, and practices, and toward monotheism or monism, in their endeavors to utilize the resources of letters, counteract the baffling ambiguities of historical time, and unify experience around secure values. In this task they achieved new levels of internal coherence for a religion, but at the expense of great disparity on many levels *between* religions. The silent concept-free meditation of Japanese Zen; the worship of Allah, the Merciful, the Compassionate, as one bows and kneels in the direction of Mecca in Egyptian Islam today; the choirs and sacraments of the Church of England with its Apostles' and Nicene Creeds—these would probably strike many observers as suggesting more diversity of ideology and practice than would the local polytheistic practices in each place of millennia ago.

Nonetheless, similarities remain as well. Unquestionably these religions all carried over much from prehistory. The old gods became saints or guardians of the new savior: the shaman's archaic ecstasy became the new mystic's trance or contemplative prayer. Most important of all, the new religions preserved the ageless awareness of the sacred, of nonmaterial reality, indeed expressing its verity in much fuller if sometimes tendentious oceans of words.

It is here that theosophy contributes to the general picture of how religion has evolved to what it is now, by adding an understanding of the meaning and truth behind all religious statements. It holds that the apperception of sacred reality underlying the visible world by primal religion is basically a true one: general belief in soul, in immortality, in divine spirits, in high gods, and in the unity of the cosmos as a vast multilevel system with a spiritual background, into which human life must be integrated. Moreover, the great initiated souls who taught doctrines out of the sacred tradition at the dawn of history, and who later founded the great religions, embodied the same essential truth under many different guises.

According to this view, although the world religions have a valid historical role to play and, most importantly, retain an esoteric kernel of truth within them, they have in some ways gone astray. This development was unavoidable. In a stage of history marked by rapidly accelerating verbalization, they became logjammed with words. At a time when human society was becoming much more complex than ever before, with compounding division of labor and fast-oxpanding political structures, they became overly institutionalized, matching massive state bureaucracies with priesthoods, and palaces with equally costly temples. As people were becoming more and more bedazzled by the increasing diversity and power of the material realm—as technology and trade burgeoned and, for some, opulence grew—it was easy to lose sight of the primal awareness of the sacred side of things. Or, what is just as bad if not worse, the sacred—"God and immortal spirit"—are treated as essentially another "material" component of human life. Spirit becomes an objective, verbalized idea, a segment of experience to be compartmentalized into its cultural cubbyhole as "the religious dimension," or the professional domain of a particular class where, for all intents and purposes, it is bought and sold like shoes.

Theosophy tries to get behind all that to say again what the great spiritual teachers said at the beginning, and have reiterated over and over. It does not

blandly say that all religions are alike or teach exactly the same thing in different words. Religious history is a more complicated matter than such easy
generalizations imply. The great religions give voice
to divine truths in specific ways to answer specific
human needs, and have played quite different historical roles, albeit they may have the same ultimate
impulse and heritage.

But theosophy does affirm just as insistently that
behind all religion lies the selfsame reality, the primal awareness of the divine Ground of being,
brought to the world as revealed truth by a Master of
Wisdom. The supreme light is refracted through
ideas and symbols, but it has to be sought; the windows through which it ought to shine may have acquired much grime and need painstakingly to be
cleaned.

The theosophical worldview also fosters an appreciation of the complexity of religious history in
another important way. That history is neither an
easy evolution to a better and better world, nor a
degeneration from a state of simple purity. Recognition of the primal awareness does not imply some
romantic idealization of early man as the "noble sav-
age" on the historical plane. Much was undeniably
brutal about his life. But at the same time his human
existence was sufficiently untrammeled that some
pristine awarenesses came more easily to him than
they do in later days. Yet the content of those awarenesses was certainly articulated more fully by the
Shankaras, the Nagarjunas, the Plotinuses of verbally
more sophisticated eras. In this respect one can trace
a positive development in religion. In things of the
spirit, we can neither say "the later, the better," nor
"the earlier, the better" in categorical terms, any
more than we can so characterize the history of art

or literature. Picasso may have painted a greater
variety of subjects and possessed more sophisticated
equipment, but to claim that he was a *better* artist
than the best of the Paleolithic cave painters would
be problematic. In religion, we have far *more* words,
concepts, and ideas about spirit and all that goes
with it than the cave-man did. We can say more
about the primal awarenesses we may both share.
But words create new problems even as they solve
others; they can get us into trouble and they can get
us out of it. They can fool us into thinking we understand ultimate things better than we do because
we've given them names: they can make simple
things look complicated and can oversimplify the
complex: they can even become missiles we hurl at
supposed enemies. Yet employed by a master who
knows that regarding supreme truths words can only
point, but that such pointers, when used with the
right delicacy, can indeed help clarify inner intuitions, they have a role.

This is a role to which theosophy wishes to aspire.
Despite a plethora of books, theosophy is fundamentally more a way of seeing than of talking, for it is
aware of language's ambivalences. It tries to take its
own words, and those of all faiths, not as dogma but
as pointers to open up spiritual vistas which extend
past language's horizon yet which words can vector.

Theosophy therefore enables one to approach the
religions of the world with neither reductionism nor
chauvinism. It does not say they are all "nothing
but" something conditioned by culture or psychol-
ogy, nor does it say they are all the same, or that one
is true and others false. They all contain spiritual
truth and the power that goes with it. Better, they all
hold the power to open up one's inner awareness of
"God and immortal spirit." Yet they must all be ap-

proached critically and without arrogating the claims of one over all others, for they all contain that treasure in earthen vessels.

The theosophist can walk the temples of the world with what must be a unique combination of appreciation and reserve. He or she can sense in the vivid riot of color and form of a Hindu temple, in the great peace of a Buddhist stupa where the world-enlightened one is honored, in the rustic charm of a Shinto shrine, or the cool, clean openness of a great Muslim mosque, not only a way to God but a particular way taught by initiated Masters and rooted in human history. They are, together with the synagogue and the Christian church, ways in which spiritual growth back to the One has been expressly and validly authorized, if one may use the term. The theosophist can love, honor, and practice any of them and all of them. At the same time, he can view them with a certain obliqueness, knowing that none can make unqualified claims or demands.

One may love a certain painting above all others, yet the hold it has on one is the hold of love; one does not insist that this painting alone contains all the beauty in the world, or that other paintings may not have a measure of loveliness as well. So with faith; one loves Jesus or the Buddha all the better for recognizing they are human expressions of that which is beyond all forms and words, for what our love most seeks is a human face. But in the end, the faiths themselves teach that to know the Buddha is to know that all sentient beings are buddhas; to love Christ is to see Christ in all—"Inasmuch as ye have done it unto the least of these my brethren, ye have done it unto me."

7
Theosophical Living

BRING IT TOGETHER

How do we apply the riches of theosophical tradition in everyday life? Most of the days we apportion ourselves are unremarkable. They are dry, quickly fade to memory, seem made up of little bits and pieces. At the same time, these small dusty weeks and years are set against the flaming backdrop of a world-as-usual too much with us, and packed with poignant hope and appalling horror. Can theosophy help us to string together our days and see the backdrop in the right perspective? If so, how do we live accordingly?

If the foregoing parts of this book are of any merit, the answer to the first question clearly is yes. Theosophy offers a worldview with two great complementary benefits for satisfactory daily living: it shows that on the one hand the time over which evolution toward the Good is taking place is immense, and on the other hand that nothing is trivial. We need therefore not become depressed at the constant setbacks we see around us, and can also be confident that everything we can do for good, however tiny, will not be lost, but will augment through its wholesome karma our own evolution and that of the world—toward unimaginable splendors to come.

Now we will look at what kind of life-thought and lifestyle theosophy enjoins as best creating that good in ways large and small. For purposes of this discussion, we shall gather the principles of theosophical living under five headings: duty, service, expression, naturalness, and fellowship. In the last analysis, though, the five are one principle—a way of seeing which is inseparable from a way of doing, wherein the one spontaneously engenders the other. For theosophy sets great store by the realization that genuine right living cannot be merely a matter of legalistic prescription but must come out of deep wisdom and compassion.

As we have seen, these two necessarily go together. If one sees all the factors of the world profoundly enough, as one can with an eye clear of ego and suffused with love, one will spontaneously know what to do to express compassion, without need of rules and regulations. Nevertheless, for those of us still young in spiritual growth, some guidelines are of help in stretching spiritual muscles and finding the way of life that best will aid the world's maturation and our own. Some of the guidelines that theosophy has presented toward these ends may be of help to you.

Duty

Classical theosophical writings emphasize the notion of *duty*. They say, in other words, that there are certain things each person is *supposed* to do in his or her life. Some may be common to all persons. But of special interest is the concept that one may have a special, personal duty—something each individual is supposed to do, something that, if one fails in this duty, will not be done and the entire world will thereby be set back by so much. For just as no two leaves or snowflakes are the same, so are no two human lives and responsibilities. Karma, the overall course of evolution, and the calling of the Masters set particular tasks before us which out of our free will we may accept or reject. We take the consequences of either choice.

The theosophical concept of duty is based on the Hindu idea of *dharma*. Dharma is a Sanskrit word related to our word "form," and embraces the general form or order of the world, with special emphasis on one's moral obligations toward society that help keep it running.

That obligation implies something else: *svadharma*, one's own personal dharma or place in the vast organism which is the world. Ancient Indian texts like the *Bhagavad-Gita*, a favorite of theosophists, give a picture of the world of conditioned reality as like a huge game in which each piece must move in accordance with its rules in order to keep the whole going smoothly. The role of each piece is determined first of all by its dharma of nation, class, sex, stage of life, and historical circumstances. Above all, traditionalists saw it in terms of the caste system of Hinduism.

Modern commentators, including theosophists, have emphasized a personal dharma, which may or may not conform to the status given one by birth. Sometimes in chess a queen must move like a pawn, and a pawn can move a short way like a queen. If a person's inner compass will not let him rest until he has done an unconventional thing, taken an unexpected stand, on behalf of what he knows is right, then that is svadharma and must be heeded. It must set one's direction not only for that individual's own sake, but also for the sake of the whole game. It may be that such a person was *meant* to break out of a conventional role because the whole game is about to escalate to another stage, and he is intended to be a pioneer rather than a follower. Duty, finally, comes from within, though the indications given by the place one finds oneself are not to be ignored either. Only the cultivation of wisdom and compassion can give sure guides, but knowing that one *has* a duty—or duties—is a good beginning.

Concerning the turning world with all its woes, theosophy takes these problems seriously but not despairingly. It is a delicate matter that requires just the right angle of vision.

The anguish of a single tormented child or animal is worth unbounded compassion and rightly causes us to ponder deeply the moral meaning of the universe. Theosophy sees these tears within the context of immense cycles through which evils will be transcended and the same child or beast, like all the rest of us, will find degrees of glory that surpass the horrors of which this world is capable. A theosophical attitude toward world history with all its ambiguity, its war and peace, was well summed up by J. J. van der Leeuw in *The Fire of Creation* as he discussed the Third Ray and the wisdom that especially goes with it.

> Characteristic of the Third Ray is the dynamic view of the universe, in which we never see a thing detached or by itself, but always as part of an evolutionary process. Thus every institution, movement, nation, or race is understood in its relation with the past that produced it, and as the cause of the future which it will in turn produce.

> This view of the universe enables us to gain a far deeper understanding of any subject under consideration . . .
>
> In political science we find forms of government discussed and judged on their own merits as if such a thing could ever be, and one form will be called better in itself than some other form. Once we have gained the standpoint of the Third Ray, we can see that each form of government is the natural product of a certain type of mentality reached by a nation in its evolution. Thus a form of government which expresses the point reached by some nation in its evolution is a right form, not right in itself, but right for that particular nation at that particular time. However, the same form which was right yesterday may become wrong today . . .
>
> Thus the Dharma of a nation at some particular time is the fitting expression of the life of that nation in its forms of government and social organization; and the Dharma of an individual will, in a similar way, be the harmonious expression in a scheme of life of the type and level of evolution manifest in that individual. (pp. 100-101)

Like all profound truths, this perspective is profoundly dangerous and profoundly liberating. It is dangerous if it leads us to be so "philosophical" about evils in governments or in our own lives that we do nothing to change them. For the whole point, as van der Leeuw makes clear, is that what establishes one thing as good for one time and place but not for another is that they all are in a process of evolution.

Once an evil is *perceived* as evil, it is no longer even a "relative" good but something that evolution is ready to do away with. If we are not part, then, of the evolutionary process that supersedes the lesser with the greater good, it is not because our wisdom is too broad but too narrow, unable to read the signs of the times. While powerful forces are behind evolution, it can never be forced on free and intelligent beings like us humans but requires our conscious consent. Not seldom this entails hard decisions to refuse the comfortable status quo, either in our society or in our own lives. Right here is where a keen sense of one's personal dharma or duty fits in.

But the perspective of relativity that van der Leeuw describes is also deeply liberating, for it helps one maintain joy and serenity and a sense of the "big picture," in the midst of short-term social or political trends that may be distressing, and may indeed be genuinely bad. Like biological evolution, social and spiritual evolutions are not "straight line" developmental patterns. One stage is not necessarily followed by something a little better. While the very long-range trend is upward, the history of the animal kingdom, and that of nations and persons, offers many examples of "dead ends," unsuccessful adaptations, and apparent retrogressions back to cruder levels. Theosophy, by constantly keeping the "big picture" before our eyes, enables us to see all this with wisdom and compassion. The wisdom keeps us calm, while the compassion goads us to do something to help get things back on the right track. Seeing the larger view ought to entail larger compassion—if it does not, it is only pseudo-wisdom.

Although individual duties or dharmas will be different, they all work together for ultimate good—the diverse tasks that each of us do, if we reckon those tasks aright, will be seen to converge at the endless end of the evolutionary trail. Each person who acted according to his or her true calling will have contributed in a unique and invaluable way to that end. Some may heal, some may teach, some may feed and nurture, some may govern, but all are to advance evolution back to the One whatever the outer conditions.

Theosophy has given us outstanding examples of persons to whom the call to dharma was a call to evolutionary change rather than to resignation. Henry Steel Olcott, despite his duties as first president of the Theosophical Society, found time to labor on behalf of the dignity and well-being of Buddhists in Ceylon (Sri Lanka) and elsewhere against the opposition one would expect in the high noon of imperialism. Annie Besant, his successor as president, fought for education and home rule in India, despite hostility from many of her British countrymen and even a brief prison term during World War I. Many other examples could be cited: the basic theme is that the particular style of wisdom and compassion which theosophy tends to nurture in its adherents is both activist and evolutionary. It has generally been on the side of freedom, democracy, education, and human rights, favoring responsible reforms in these directions. Knowing that change is always happening in an evolutionary universe, yet also that we humans can have much to say about what kind of change takes place on our own level, theosophists seek to "push" change in helpful directions, while avoiding those radical and revolutionary stances which, being nonevolutionary, have a way of backfiring.

Beyond this, little should be said about the role of theosophists in society, for different people work in different ways and from different directions, perhaps meeting only far, far down the road. The Theosophical Society itself traditionally takes no stand on most social or political issues, and members from presidents on down who do so—as many have—are careful to distinguish these activities from their role in the Society and not to implicate the Society as such in them.

SERVICE

The actual expression of duty is in service, another frequently used term in theosophy. Just as duty derives from dharma, so service in theosophical usage is based on the karma-yoga inculcated by the *Bhagavad-Gita*. There Krishna taught Arjuna that liberation could be realized by the person working in the world as surely as by the yogin in his cave, if that person did the work for the sake of duty, as it were, by proxy for the divine within, not out of attachment to the fruits of the work. Service, then, is work done for its own sake, because it is good and one's obligation, not because one hopes to get something out of it, whether material reward or the esteem of others or even inner gratification of an egocentric sort. In the theosophical context, service is work done for the benefit of others, whether human or beast, and thus an expression of compassion and a "push" along the evolutionary upward trail.

The "inner asceticism" of karma-yoga, which focuses strictly on the rightness of the act itself and not on its results, can be wonderfully releasing for a person with a lively sense of duty, one who feels that something that is right must be said or done, whether it is in season or out. Motivated by karma-yoga, one is unconcerned with whether a thing is currently fashionable or not, whether it will succeed—at least in one's own lifetime—whether it will bring one praise and fame, or opprobrium and perhaps even persecution and death. Not a few people, so motivated, have suffered seeming failure in their own lives, yet sowed the seeds of developments for good harvested by later generations. At the same time, the abeyance of ego which is the heart of karma-yoga (and theosophical wisdom) should also free one from impulsiveness and bestow a sense of evolutionary timing, for in all work for good the Third Ray gift of correct time and place is crucial.

What kind of service should one do? This is an inner matter. Some may find the service to which they are called largely in their vocation, as we have seen, as teacher, doctor, nurse, counselor. Even those whose work appears on the surface to be less service-oriented than these can still be servants: to do a good, conscientious job as bricklayer or TV repairman is also service, and all jobs provide opportunity to spread good will among fellow-workers and those one meets by a friendly smile and a helping hand.

Whether to seek a more service-oriented job or to dedicate oneself to doing good where one is, only the individual can decide after honest reflection. But there are some guidelines for those faced with such a decision. Don't foreclose the possibility that you may be called to change your work, and don't overlook the possibility of doing more where you are. Never assume that you *can't* be like the greatest of those dedicated to service, an Albert Schweitzer, a Gandhi, a Mother Teresa. You haven't lived all your life yet, and no one really knows what his or her fullest potentials are. If the dream of a great adventure in service like theirs is stirring within you, don't let fear or lethargy get the best of you. But if you honestly are convinced that where you are is best for you, give yourself unstintingly to it.

Some find the call to service is best met by whole-hearted labor for the Theosophical Society; the

Society depends on those who work for it for little or no monetary reward. Others do volunteer work outside of their jobs in all sorts of capacities such as in hospitals and for charitable organizations. Anyone who is really looking for a way to serve humanity will soon find one that is right.

While theosophists certainly applaud any worthwhile form of service, certain causes have traditionally been particularly favored by them as especially significant in light of theosophical teaching. In addition to the usual forms of humanitarianism, these include work for education, human rights, and animal welfare.

It is not surprising that theosophists should put emphasis on education since theosophy stresses mental and spiritual growth, and its comprehension requires some intellectual effort. In India, Sri Lanka, and elsewhere theosophists have been instrumental in founding educational institutions from the primary to university levels, and not a few theosophists are in the teaching professions.

Likewise, the great stress that theosophy puts on human brotherhood and its root rationale, the fact that all persons are eternal Pilgrims and expressions of the divine within, justifies the importance the tradition has given to work for the equal treatment of all regardless of race, sex, or creed. Closely related are traditional concerns for prisoners, the blind, and children.

Animals, too, are sentient and share the divine nature. For this reason, and from out of that compassion which is inseparable from wisdom, theosophists have long felt a special commitment to the welfare of animals. Many are vegetarian, partly for compassionate reasons, and many are involved in programs to reduce or eliminate the suffering of animals in research institutes, slaughterhouses, pounds, and farms. The "holistic" view of the world that theosophy tends to encourage, with its emphasis on the interdependence of all life, also leads many to a concern for appropriate preservation of nature and a responsible human attitude toward ecology and the environment. It may be recognized, for example, that on a small overpopulated planet, many more people can be fed a healthy vegetarian diet than can be adequately nourished when grain production is wastefully diverted into feed for meat-producing animals.

Theosophy inculcates that direct, personal service is best. Helena Blavatsky, in *The Key to Theosophy*, wrote:

> The Theosophical ideas of charity mean *personal* exertion for others; *personal* mercy and kindness; *personal* interest in the welfare of those who suffer; *personal* sympathy, forethought and assistance in their troubles or needs. We Theosophists do not believe in giving money...through other people's hands or organizations. We believe in giving to the money a thousandfold greater power and effectiveness by our personal contact and sympathy with those who need it. (p. 244)

This statement presumably should not be taken to mean one ought never to give money to good causes with which one cannot become personally involved, or should never work for political or social reforms which one believes will in the end reduce suffering by alleviating some of its underlying sources. But the main point is well taken. Much evidence shows that those theosophists like Olcott and Besant who were involved in social reform were also very much engaged with needy persons in highly personal ways. Far too often we seek to do good only at a distance, antiseptically, knowing little and possibly caring less

about the "real people" concerned. But as Mother
Teresa has so vividly illustrated in her life, the sick
and destitute need the love which can only be communicated by "personal contact and sympathy" as
much or more than they need medicine and food;
the best service is personally present and gives both
together.

EXPRESSION

Now we come to a quite different facet of theosophical living. Theosophical notions have long been an
inspiration to the arts. Poets like William Butler
Yeats and George Russell (AE), painters like Piet
Mondrian and Nicholas Roerich, and composers like
Aleksandr Scriabin have given artistic expression to
theosophical ideas. The grand vistas in space and
time, the cycles great and small, the idea of thought-
forms and the lore of initiations—all are well able to
impel the artist to express in the magic of verse, col-
or, or sound that which is beyond the holding-power
of ordinary language.

Anyone who feels drawn by theosophical ideas
should let them help in writing, painting, or compos-
ing. Not all of us will or should be professionals in
these areas, but a good theosophical life can be multi-
dimensional, and amateurs can serve their souls as
well through brush, pen, or piano as can professionals—some might argue better. The theosophical view
of human nature, in which image-ideas brought over
from Devachan can be the seeds of new creations,
makes artistic work especially important. For it is
not seldom through such expression that fresh ideas
or visions first find their way into our dimensions of
space, time, and mind. Just as importantly, the arts
can also concretize and so begin to make real,

especially for those without clairvoyant gifts, the nature of the etheric, astral, and mental worlds in which color and thought-forms are so revelatory.

For the theosophist, then, the arts are not to be neglected. They should be a significant dimension in the life of one aware of the "inner planes" and seeking their full integration into outer life. Also important to theosophists, one might add, is sensitivity to psychic energies—those latent powers demonstrated in telepathy, clairvoyance, or healing—so long as the attention one gives them is responsible and balanced.

NATURALNESS

I had first thought to name this section "discipline," with the intention of bringing out that a theosophical lifestyle requires some self-control to keep itself in tune with the truest theosophical ideals. So it does, as must any life oriented toward duty, service, and artistic expression. So also must any life oriented toward transcendent goals and the coequal reality of spirit and matter.

The immediate sensory gratification the material can offer, and the symbolic importance it has in an affluent consumer society, means that to keep to those ideals one must often restrain impulses grounded in the "pleasure principle." With even greater firmness, one must deal with those passions grounded in the mind, or that more or less astral level at which we are much taken by images speaking to our pretensions as to sophistication, social class, income level, and the like.

Despite the clear-eyed self-control side of it, on further reflection I came to feel that the spirit of theosophical living is less well expressed in the word "discipline" than the term "naturalness." For the latter expression means, of course, following a way that is in accordance with nature, with the way things really are. It means living as what we human beings are truly, in the universe as it is. If the theosophical worldview has any validity, then, it means giving due place to consciousness and spirit, and recognizing as unnatural delusions the call of the material senses and the passion-laden astral fantasies—when they would have us act as if they were all there is.

Our purpose in this fourth-globe world is to experience the material level fully but not to get trapped in it. A simple life is the most natural, for it appreciates the best of matter expressed in nature, art, and person—without getting lost in the false materiality, really lower astral attraction, of money and sensuality. For such things as money, prestige, status, and compulsive hedonism are not grounded in nature but in twisted passions of the mind and emotions. They are really abstractions, symbols, rather than the "hard" naturalism of wholesome food, the beauty of trees and sky, and human warmth.

As a part of living naturally, many theosophists are vegetarians and do not use tobacco, alcohol, and nonmedicinal drugs. Meat and the latter substances are not necessary to a complete human life, nor are they grounded in any biological need. They are, rather, physical components, substitutes for spiritual incompleteness, ways in which the mind tries to give itself power, energy, and ecstasy—or the symbols thereof—that it has been unable to draw from the spiritual side directly. They are, moreover, likely to be physically harmful. Consciously or unconsciously to harm the physical body is no way to show that appreciation of the material plane which we are to develop in this globe.

However, it must be emphasized that theosophy lays down no law on such matters. Its morality is not a matter of legalistic "do's and don'ts" but is based on awareness that morality must grow out of spiritual maturation, which will occur at varying rates and in varying ways. No position or practice regarding vegetarianism, smoking, drinking, or drugs is a condition of membership in the Theosophical Society, although meals served at theosophical centers or meetings are invariably vegetarian and alcohol-free. Theosophists from the founders on down have pursued a diversity of patterns in their personal lives on these issues, and no condemnation of anyone is expressed.

The important thing is that one set up priorities based on the reality of the spiritual as well as the material side of nature, and strive to be truly natural in a muddled world. As with the whole spectrum of theosophy, different people will find different ideas of theosophy more meaningful to them than others and will vary in "what they are ready for" at different stages of life. Some theosophical teachers hold out the ideal of freedom from meat, tobacco, alcohol, and nonmedicinal drugs as parts of a genuinely natural life; one's response can only be a very personal matter, toward which no one else has a right to be judgmental.

Another area of living in which genuine naturalness is an important touchstone is sexuality. Some might, I suppose, imagine that people as given to the "spiritual" as theosophists would regard the sexual drive as little more than carnal nature, to be suppressed as much as possible. Such an attitude, however, would indicate small understanding of the deep interaction of spirit and matter, in which each is a symbol participating in the other, or of our calling on this globe and above all in the Fifth Race, to *authentic* expression of all the glory of which the material realm is capable.

Authentic sexuality is in no way a false material-ism really worshipping an abstraction or mental fan-tasy, like some we have mentioned, but a miracle close to the very heart of the creative splendor of which spirit-matter is capable. An international president of the Theosophical Society, George S. Arundale, expressed this view very well in an article called "The Glory of Sex" (*The Theosophist*, Adyar, LXI, 11, August 1940). He wrote, "The urge of sex, as we call it, though it has been so degraded every-where, means in fact the Creative Spirit of God . . . . There is no doubt that the sex urge is the nearest force we have to that Godliness which is essentially ours . . . .To draw nearer to our essential Godliness or to create like a God, or to do both, that is the purpose, the objective of the sexual urge."

The very divinity in the power of sex, needless to say, gives it a special potential for evil. When it is falsely associated with the ego rather than the divine within, it can serve as an instrument for the exploita-tion of others and gratification of the false gods with-in oneself of status, pride, or hedonistic pleasure. As a divine power, it can be properly used only in a way which respects the divine freedom and essence of all concerned: male, female, and potential child. It must only fulfill itself completely in the context of liberty, love, and marital commitment. But when it does so, it is one shining facet of the material glory we have come to this globe to experience in the course of the great pilgrimage.*

---

*We do not mean to imply that sexuality need be experienced physically for one to know the creative divine energy it bears. Arundale meant by sexuality a broadly understood life-energy which can easily, in the language of psychoanalysis, be sublimated quite properly into other areas of expression. Many people, including many theosophists, have well served the Creative Spirit of God on the special level of freedom and commitment that celibacy affords.

FELLOWSHIP

Theosophy can be studied when one is alone, and many people may transit times when that is what they feel drawn to do. We humans are social creatures, however, and most of us sooner or later will want to express ideas and values that are truly important to us by associating with other people of like mind, and perhaps identifying with institutions designed to perpetuate them. For these reasons many for whom the study and practice of theosophy has come to have an important role in life choose to become involved in the life of the Theosophical Society. Our discussion would not be complete without a few words concerning this unique organization.

The Theosophical Society is not a church or religion in the usual sense; many theosophists, including myself, are also members of a church or other religious organization. Theosophists include Christians, Hindus, Buddhists, and others. There is no suggestion that one must formally become a theosophist to be "saved" or receive special grace. Three reasons for affiliating with the Society, however, present themselves.

1. *Support of one another.* People need sometimes to be in the company of those who are like-minded, to encourage and support each other. We must frankly acknowledge that in some circles in our larger society theosophical views are not well understood or regarded; in such circumstances it helps to know that one is not alone and to talk over the experience of being a theosophist in today's world.

2. *Learning.* Most theosophical activities on both local and higher levels basically center around studying and learning more about the vast and deep theosophical tradition, whether through lectures, films, or discussions—although theosophists do take

time out once in a while just to have fun in dinners, parties, or excursions. Most people learn better with others—listening to someone who is particularly well prepared on a certain topic or discussing and learning from the questions and experiences of others inevitably enhances our own understanding.

3. *Aiding theosophical work.* In the world as it is, any worthwhile labor to promote important ideas and values is greatly assisted by an institutional structure. It requires money, specialized talents, buildings, and mailings. All this is what well-set-up institutions can provide. It goes without saying that institutionalization can bring problems. Institutions can become rigid; ideas can become dogmas; people, being human, can become attached to status within the institution. Yet without structures important messages like that of theosophy are easily drowned out by the clamor of those which do have well-heeled institutions, and unsupported knowledge can be blown away by the high winds of history as generations pass and books go out of print. Theosophists have, with some exceptions, considered that institutionalization on some levels of the work is essential and have determined to make the institutions as good as they can. The earlier literature emphasizes that the Masters themselves have elected to work through the Society in the world and that work for it is one of the best forms of service.

Throughout a colorful history of over a century, which will be briefly traced in Appendix A, the Theosophical Society has not always avoided the dangers attendant upon institutionalization. But it has survived and has, I believe it is fair to say, now arrived at a point where it is doing reasonably effective work and has struck a balance between the crucial mission of preserving its distinctive teachings and excessive rigidity. Many members find life in the Society a joy: it is filled with interesting and stimulating people, is truly an international community wherein one can make friends around the world, and maintains schools and conference centers in some extraordinarily beautiful and "spiritual" settings.

We shall now look somewhat more specifically at the life and work of the Theosophical Society. Our model will be the Theosophical Society in America, and the international Theosophical Society headquartered at Adyar, Madras, India. At least two other Theosophical Societies exist, plus a number of groups which have sprung from or been considerably influenced by the theosophical movement. Most of them are doing good work. We will look at the historical circumstances behind this diversity in the Appendix. But members attached to "Adyar" Theosophy are the most numerous, and this group has by far the largest number of branches in the United States and around the world.

The basic local unit is the branch, formerly sometimes called the lodge, or the smaller study center. These are chartered by the national organization and are comprised of members of the Society in the area who wish to be members of the branch rather than members-at-large. The local branch is governed in an entirely democratic way, officers being elected by the membership. Some have their own buildings. Activities consist of holding meetings which are generally lectures, films, or discussion relevant to theosophy, occasional social activities, and selling or distributing theosophical literature, largely at meetings, though there are a few full-time book shops.

Some regional theosophical structures have been organized. However, the next important level is the national: the Theosophical Society in America, or in Canada, England, India, or some forty-five other national "sections." The American society is governed by a president, two vice-presidents, and a board of six directors, all elected by the membership by mail ballot for terms. The national headquarters is located on spacious and beautiful grounds in the Chicago suburb of Wheaton, Illinois. Here is found a fine library, the Theosophical Publishing House, which puts out Quest Books, a bookstore, and the offices of the national periodical, *The American Theosophist,* as well as administrative facilities, and rooms and dining halls for guests.

Additional work of the national organization includes that of the Department of Education, which prepares study material, including correspondence courses in theosophy; the distribution of radio programs and audio-cassettes; a program for prisoners; and the Theosophical Research Institute, which studies the second and third objectives of the Society. Links between the national headquarters and local branches are maintained not only by correspondence and periodicals, but also by visits to branches of the national president and a national lecturer. The headquarters at Wheaton is something of a theosophical community, for a number of workers there live in homes, rooms, and apartments on the grounds.

The Theosophical Order of Service, founded by Annie Besant in 1908, is a related organization. In America it is efficiently organized into departments dealing with such traditional areas of theosophical concern as animal welfare, arts and music, ecology, healing, parenting, peace, social service, and Tibetan friendship.

Another important center is the Krotona Institute and School of Theosophy, located in the lovely town of Ojai, California. It is basically a school and library, wherein classes in theosophical topics are given year-round, attracting students from all over the world. Nearby is a theosophical retirement community.

Theosophists also maintain some five camps in various parts of the country which draw many visitors during the summer. The experience of thinking about theosophy in these spectacular seaside or mountaintop environments does much to deepen the meaning of the tradition and build theosophical friendships among those who find their way to them.

As we have seen, the Theosophical Society in America is but one of some forty-five national sections, though the second largest after India. The international headquarters is on the southern edge of the city of Madras in southern India, on quiet, ample grounds bordering the Indian Ocean and the wide, slow-moving Adyar River. This establishment, rich in historical associations for theosophists, contains residences, memorials, a museum, an auditorium, and a library world-famous for research facilities in Indic studies as well as theosophy, together with offices.

We might conclude our survey of the structures of theosophical life with just a mention of the Esoteric School, a group within the Society founded by Helena Blavatsky and devoted to special programs of study, inner work, and the consistent following of a Theosophical lifestyle.

We see, then, that theosophy encompasses three things. It is an *attitude* of openness toward infinity and that which transcends the power of words to express. It is, however, also a *set of ideas* which undogmatically endeavors to communicate something of the inner nature of infinite reality, its relation to consciousness, and its evolutionary process. It is finally a *lifestyle* which seeks to be both truly natural and worthy of living in such a wondrous universe, shaped by wisdom and compassion.

APPENDIX A

A Brief History of Modern Theosophy

While theosophy has ancient roots, its modern presence in the world under this name is largely associated with the Theosophical Society founded in New York in 1875 and the literature related to it. A grasp of this history is not necessary to an appreciation of theosophical ideas, but it is a fascinating story and helps to set them in context.

The early segments of the narrative center around two persons, Helena Petrovna Blavatsky (1831-91) and Henry Steel Olcott (1832-1907). A greater contrast between two whose lives became so deeply interlinked in a single work could not easily be imagined. Helena Blavatsky was a woman born of high aristocracy in the old Russia of czars and onion-domed churches. A strong-willed and imaginative child, she impetuously married N.V. Blavatsky, a widower more than twice her age, at only sixteen, but soon separated from him. The next twenty-five years were spent in extensive travel. According to her own account, she searched about the world for the secrets behind occult lore, as she was more and more insistently drawn by the call of two Masters of the Wisdom, M. (Morya) and K.H. (Kuthumi), who realized that she had unique gifts as a potential transmitter of the ancient wisdom to a modern world desparately in need of it. Those wandering and hidden years culminated in her receiving certain initiations in Tibet which enabled her to fulfill that vocation. In 1874, under further instructions from her Masters, she came to the United States.

There, at the site of spiritualistic manifestations in Vermont which interested them both, she met Henry Olcott. Coming from the sturdy middle class of democratic America, Olcott was a popular writer on scientific agriculture, an investigator of fraudulent military suppliers for the Union during the Civil War, and sometime dabbler in the spiritualism which was a mid-nineteenth-century vogue in America. After the war he made a career for himself in New York as a lawyer and journalist; it was in the latter capacity that he went to Vermont and met the intriguing immigrant from Russia.

Upon their return to New York, Olcott (estranged from his wife and later divorced) and Blavatsky became fast companions. Gradually the enigmatic Russian woman revealed to him her mysterious powers and introduced him to the Masters of the Wisdom. All this is delightfully recorded in Olcott's *Old Diary Leaves*. Their apartment, dubbed the "Lamasery," became a magnet for New York's coterie of independent thinkers and spiritual seekers. It was the scene of lectures on esoteric mysteries, wonderful discussions, and lively parties, all presided over by the unforgettable Blavatsky with her exotic accent, sharp tongue, and aura of being mediator of mysteries.

Toward the end of 1875 several people of the Lamasery crowd determined to form an organization devoted to the sort of studies in which they were engaged. Thus the Theosophical Society was formally inaugurated on November 17, 1875, with Olcott as first president and Blavatsky as corresponding secretary. (Though she was certainly catalyst of the movement, that was the only formal office in it she ever held.) Other early members included William Q. Judge, later president of the American section and a leading theosophical writer; Thomas Edison, the great inventor; and General Abner Doubleday, according to tradition developer of the game of baseball.

The nascent society, however, sustained vital life for only a few months in this period. As if in compensation, Blavatsky and an inner circle, including Olcott, then devoted major attention to her first large-scale publication,

Isis Unveiled, which came out in 1877. Shortly after the book's unexpected success, the "Theosophical Twins," as Olcott liked to call himself and Blavatsky, felt led to transfer to India, supreme reservoir in the present-day world of the ancient wisdom. This they did, arriving in early 1879. At first their headquarters were in Bombay, but in late 1882 it was established on the spacious estates at Adyar, near Madras, where the international headquarters is still located.

Olcott and Blavatsky traveled extensively about India in those years, making a notable impact on both the European and the native communities. The Theosophical Society grew rapidly. Native Indians particularly appreciated the great respect its outlook afforded their traditional religion and culture, so much at variance with the attitude conveyed by many Westerners in the heyday of imperialism. As we have seen, Olcott concerned himself with the welfare of Buddhists in Ceylon and elsewhere, interceding on their behalf with colonial officials. It was in the early 1880s that the "Mahatma Letters" were communicated to A.P. Sinnett, sometime editor of an important English newspaper in India, the *Allahabad Pioneer*, and later writer of major theosophical books.

In 1884, however, a difficult period in theosophical life commenced, with charges by certain associates of Blavatsky at Adyar, abetted by Christian missionaries, that some of her "phenomena," especially the "precipitation" of letters from the Masters, was fraudulent. A later investigation by a representative of the Society for Psychical Research in England went with the charges. Many theosophists then and since have insisted that the episode, which generated a highly emotional atmosphere, had its "witch-hunt" aspects and that the jury is still out on the true facts. At the same time, they would say that theosophical teachings as such, including the *Mahatma Letters* themselves, are not dependent on any particular view of this case. Helena Blavatsky, now in poor health, left India in 1885 to write *The Secret Doctrine* in Europe. After residing in Germany and Belgium, she finally settled in London, where she died in 1891.

Not more than a few years before her death, Helena

Blavatsky had met two persons who were to dominate the next generation of theosophists, Charles W. Leadbeater in 1884 and Annie Besant five years later. Leadbeater had been a clergyman of the Church of England and Besant married to one, though later she attained prominence as a freethinker. Both, however, eagerly embraced theosophy and quickly began active careers of writing and speaking on its behalf. Like so many early theosophists, they were vigorous, controversial, outspoken persons who made an impact on their age, both in the Society and outside it.

Annie Besant began a long tenure as president of the Society upon Olcott's death in 1907. Aided by her clairvoyant faculties and those of Leadbeater, she and her generation within the "Adyar" Society tended to emphasize a style of theosophy which described with some precision the subtle planes and the hierarchies of Masters. Annie Besant, however, also found time to work energetically for education, human welfare, and home rule in India. She and Leadbeater, together with many others, promoted the career of the distinguished spiritual teacher Jiddu Krishnamurti, in whom they believed a coming World Teacher might find a suitable vessel. In 1929 Krishnamurti rejected all formal institutions, including the Theosophical Society and groups within it he had formerly headed, and all spiritual titles. In the end, most theosophists came to realize this move was best for him and his particular mission.

Theosophy has been mother to a number of movements and organizations in addition to Krishnamurti's. The first division goes back to 1895 when the Society in the United States, under William Q. Judge, declared itself independent of the Adyar headquarters. Later, under the leadership of Katherine Tingley, this organization established an impressive theosophical community at Point Loma, in San Diego, California. It dissolved all other lodges throughout the country, so they or their successors generally returned to the Adyar connection. The Point Loma community survived until 1942, when it was moved under financial and wartime exigencies. It now has a headquarters and excellent library in Altadena, near Los Angeles, and works largely through periodicals and publications without official branches.

A third group, the United Lodge of Theosophists, was founded in 1909 by Robert Crosbie. It is relatively small but has lodges around the world. It is noted for maintaining a particularly pure form of early theosophical teaching. Both the ULT and the Point Loma Theosophical Society have served as refuges for some persons discontented with the direction of "Adyar" theosophy in the twentieth century or even before.

Other movements related to theosophy can only be named. Some, like Co-Masonry and the Liberal Catholic Church, have maintained close though unofficial ties with the Theosophical Society and have had considerable overlapping membership. Others, ranging from Anthroposophy and the Arcane School of Alice Bailey to "I Am" and its derivatives, have, often in the guise of new revelations from the Masters, presented teaching that is distinctive yet shows clear theosophical influence in style and content.

Since the 1930s, the Theosophical Society (Adyar) has progressed quietly. An era passed with the end of the Krishnamurti episode and the passing of Annie Besant and C. W. Leadbeater in 1933 and 1934 respectively. New challenges faced the Society and the world. Perhaps it was a sign of growing maturity that no further extraordinary internal problems troubled the Society. At the same time, the needs of the outer world were never greater. George Arundale, international president from 1933 until 1945, labored mightily for world peace and the triumph of right in a dark period of depression, totalitarianism, and war. The concern of theosophists for international and interracial brotherhood, freedom of thought, and human dignity was not appreciated by all. Theosophists were persecuted harshly by Nazis in Germany and occupied Europe. Nor have they been able to work openly in the Soviet Union or most of the Communist world.

Elsewhere, theosophy has maintained itself, particularly in the United States, Great Britain, the British Commonwealth countries, India, and increasingly Africa and Latin

America. Its growth has not usually been spectacular, but its influence on intellectual and spiritual life has been notably on the upswing since mid-century. Especially since the 1960s, a growing interest in the convergence of science and mysticism, in comparative religions, and in natural lifestyles has fitted well with the theosophical tradition. The Society has drawn a new class of members and friends which augurs well for the future.

Theosophical Classics

Here I wish to name and briefly discuss some of the most important books associated with the modern theosophical tradition. At the outset, let me indicate that this list is circumscribed by two conditions. First, it is limited to books deriving from the first two generations of modern theosophy, and second, it is limited to books by theosophists and so represents an "inside" point of view. Many books of great value have been written by theosophists since the end of the second generation around the early 1930s, but they do not define the tradition in quite the same way as was the privilege of those before them.

A number of books by nontheosophists have discussed the movement. Some have shown great sensitivity, and others appear affected, at least in the eyes of theosophists, by misunderstanding or even outright malice. However, this does not seem the place to critique them. Our hope is that readers wishing to strengthen their knowledge of theosophy will first allow theosophy to speak for itself through its most important books. Here they are.

H.P. Blavatsky, as we have already noted, is regarded by all modern theosophical movements as the most important theosophical writer and teacher of the modern era. Her two principal works are *Isis Unveiled* (1877) and *The Secret Doctrine* (1888). These two long books, now usually in two or more volumes each, have a very special place in theosophical literature in that they are regarded as being composed under the inspiration and guidance of Masters of the Wisdom. This is a matter the reader must judge for himself or herself, and in any case it should not be taken to mean the books are infallible on any ordinary level of understanding; as we have seen, Blavatsky herself did not claim this but hinted that in some cases she could deal only in partial or allegorical statements and her works might even contain "blinds." Nonetheless, these books are the chief original source for the theosophical worldview today, as it has been presented in the present book. While not everyone will find it easy to read those massive tomes straight through, all seriously interested in that worldview must make their acquaintance and dip into them time and time again.

Indeed, repeated plunges may well be the best way to read *Isis Unveiled* and *The Secret Doctrine*. Many readers find these singular works remarkable in their capacity not only to communicte a "surface" meaning, but at the same time to call up within the reader's mind inner vistas of beauty and meaning which go far beyond what the text itself says. Such insight is catalyzed by Blavatsky's inimitable forceful, pungent, yet evocative style. Often the ideas in these books are on the far horizon of what is comprehensible by the human mind at its ordinary working level today. Such ideas seem to reflect in dim but tantalizing tints wonders beyond that horizon, or to enchant into life deep memories and anticipations lost to everyday mind. To enter these volumes is like swimming—one enters an element not our accustomed habitat, which we must get used to and which can distort perception and motion. But it can carry us somewhere, and in the process give an exhilarating experience of another dimension.

The first book, *Isis Unveiled*, at first glance may seem mainly an account of odd magical and psychical phenomena, often in out-of-the-way places, together with vigorous and frequently quite sophisticated jabs at the foibles of establishment science and religion. In the end, though, we see that a worldview emerges behind all these presentations which in turn is a preparation for fully developed theosophy. The book is saying that there is more than materialism as ordinarily understood. Besides matter, the universe contains a spiritual force, and consciousness from which they both stem and which, on the human level, is a mingling of both.

The Secret Doctrine, accounted the most important single source by virtually all theosophists, goes on to discuss at length the inner working of spirit, matter, and consciousness in the evolution of the world and the peopling of the earth; the scenario it unfolds is fundamentally what has been presented much more briefly in this book. For a fascinating account of the inspiration and writing of The Secret Doctrine, which gives an unparalleled glimpse into the character of Helena Blavatsky, see Countess Constance Wachtmeister et al., Reminiscences of H.P. Blavatsky and The Secret Doctrine (1893, reprint 1976). An equally interesting report on the writing of Isis Unveiled is offered by Henry Steel Olcott in his Old Diary Leaves (1895-1906), Series I; the entire six volumes of Old Diary Leaves are an invaluable (and entertaining) source for early theosophical history and ideas, though Volume I may be the most intriguing.

Other basic books by H.P. Blavatsky are The Key to Theosophy (1889), a lucid presentation of essential concepts, and The Voice of the Silence (1889), said to be a translation of an ancient text, a short mystical devotional work of rare beauty. The letters, articles, and other writings of Blavatsky are numerous and of unfailing interest; they have been published in a multivolume series called Collected Writings, by the Theosophical Publishing House.

Another early theosophical writer is A.P. Sinnett, author of The Occult World (1881), a narrative of his experiences in India with Blavatsky and the Masters, and Esoteric Buddhism (1883), a fuller account of occult wisdom which anticipates many themes of The Secret Doctrine. Sinnett was also the recipient of the Mahatma Letters, those celebrated missives published as transcribed and compiled by A.T. Barker in The Mahatma Let-

ters to A.P. Sinnett (1923). Often regarded as third in theosophical importance after Blavatsky's two main works, since they also are ascribed to the Masters, the letters present incisive views on a number of topics, often informed by a strikingly realistic, modern outlook. It must be remembered, however, that these letters are slanted to answer questions put by the correspondent. They do not therefore present a step-by-step exposition of theosophy and at times may seem difficult or one-sided. But they contain remarkable insights.

Of a more contemplative nature are two other small gems of early theosophy beloved by many followers of the tradition: Mabel Collins, *Light on the Path* (1885); and Alcyone (J. Krishnamurti), *At the Feet of the Master* (1910). Another early and valuable explication of theosophical teaching, offering, like all such, the particular perspective of one deep student, is W.Q. Judge, *The Ocean of Theosophy* (1893). A work of great value to serious students is by a leader of the Point Loma community, G. de Purucker, *The Esoteric Tradition* (2 vols., 1935).

The most influential writers of "Adyar" theosophy's "second generation" were Annie Besant and C.W. Leadbeater. We have already noted their special emphases. Both wrote many books, many based on their extensive lectures and classes; we can give only a few representative titles. Perhaps the best-known books of Annie Besant, and the best introductions to her approach, are *The Ancient Wisdom: An Outline of Theosophical Teachings* (1897), *Esoteric Christianity* (1898), *A Study in Consciousness* (1904), and *Thought Power* (1903).

Popular books by C.W. Leadbeater include *Thought-Forms* (with Annie Besant; 1901), *Man Visible and Invisible* (1902), *The Inner Life* (1912), *The Hidden Side of Things* (1913), *The Masters and the Path* (1925), and *The Chakras* (1927).

Almost all books cited in this bibliography are in print and can be obtained from The Theosophical Publishing House (Box 270, Wheaton, IL 60189), from Quest Bookshops, or from theosophical or major other libraries.

Index

Alcoyne. *See At the Feet
of the Master;*
Krishnamurti, Jiddu
Alexandrian, a Mas-
ter, 139
*American Theosophist,
The,* described, 208
Arundale, George S.,
quoted on sexual-
ity, 204
Aryan Root Race. *See*
Fifth Root Race
Astral globe and sheath,
after death, 109-111; as
bodies of lunar pitris,
80-82; described, 70,
74-75; in humans, 103
Astral shell, defined, 115
At the Feet of the Master,
quoted, 123; described,
220
Atlantean Root Race,
discussed, 91-93
Atma-Sat, as First
Logos, 65
Aura, defined, 115

Besant, Annie, founder of
the Theosophical Order
of Service, 208; life,
214; works, 220
Bhagavad-Gita, men-
tioned, 191
Binary nature of reality,
discussed, 150-51
Blavatsky, Helena P.,
founder of Esoteric
School, 209; life,

211-13; quoted on
allegory in Esoteric
Teaching , 160; on
Atlanteans, 92; on birth
of the universe, 40; on
"blinds," 149; on
decline of religion, 175;
on fundamental proposi-
tions, 20; on govern-
ance of the universe
from within outwards,
30; on illusion, 26; on
intuitive knowledge of
God, 29-30; on magic,
155; on masters, 136;
on no intrinsic racial
superiority or inferior-
ity, 94-95; on oneness
of truth and religion,
167; on Parabrahman,
36-37; on personal ser-
vice, 199; on prophecy,
164-65; on reality,
28-29; on spirit and
matter as aspects of the
One, 57; on universal
process, 26; on unity of
soul and Oversoul,
30-31; works discussed,
217-19. *See also*
Judaism; Kabbala
Bowen, Robert, quotation
of Blavatsky on jnana-
yoga, 27-28
Brahman, as divine in all
things, 6
Buddha, the, in history,
177-78, 180; as master
of Second Ray, 141; as

221